The Book of American Trade Marks/8
The Annual of Trade Mark Design

David E. Carter

Book Design
Marigail Sexton

Second Printing, 1984
Third Printing, 1988

No design in this book may be copied
without the permission of the owner
of the mark.

©Copyright, 1983, Art Direction Book Co.

ART DIRECTION BOOK COMPANY
10 East 39th Street
New York, New York 10016

212/889-6500

Library of Congress Catalog Card Number: 72-76493
International Standard Book Number: 0-910158-94-0
ISBN for Standing Orders for this series: 0-910158-38-X

How to submit marks for future volumes.

This book is part of a series which shows good examples of contemporary design of trade marks, corporate symbols and logos.

Designers are invited to submit marks for possible inclusion in future volumes. Work submitted must adhere to the following guidelines:

(1) marks must be sent in the actual size they are to be reproduced in the book. Any marks not meeting this standard will be eliminated from consideration.

(2) do not mount the work.

(3) include the name of the client, and the one name to appear in the credit line as designer.

(4) send a letter giving permission for the marks to be included in the book.

Due to the large amount of material received each year, it is impossible for us to acknowledge receipt of marks.

All material should be sent to: David E. Carter, Trades Marks, P.O. Box 591, Ashland, Kentucky 41101.

7391

7395

7392

7396

7393

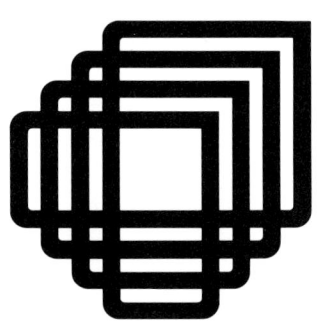

7397

7394

7398

7399

7400

7401

7391	Greenberg and Greenberg Architects Designer: Connie Asher	
7392	The Denver Triathlon Designer: Connie Asher	
7393	The Ansbury Company Designer: Connie Asher	
7394	Haley-Roth Medical Equipment, Inc. Designer: Connie Asher	
7395	The Automated Hospital Designer: Connie Asher	
7396	Guaranty Bank Designer: Connie Asher	
7397	Colorado Business Telephone Designer: Connie Asher	
7398	Builder's Etc. Designer: Connie Asher	
7399	The Great Foot Race Designer: Connie Asher	
7400	Occasions Designer: Connie Asher	
7401	Drum Corps International/Montreal 1981 Designer: Connie Asher	

7402

**Baton Rouge
Athletic & Racquet Club**

7405

7403

The Research Group

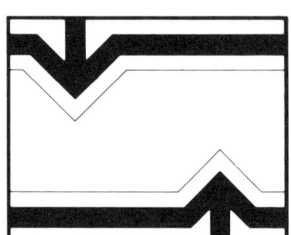

7406

7407

7404

Richard Columbus

7408

7409

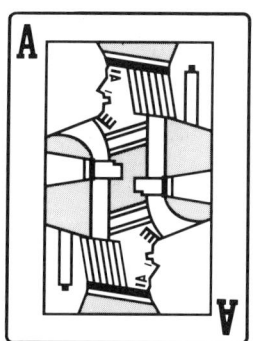

7410

7402	Baton Rouge Athletic & Racquet Club	Designer: Carlos M. Segura Jr.
7403	The Research Group	Designer: Carlos M. Segura Jr.
7404	Columbus Day	Designer: Micheal Puckett
7405	World Wide Locations	Designer: Micheal Puckett
7406	Cody	Designer: Micheal Puckett
7407	DPI Labs	Designer: Carlos M. Segura Jr.
7408	Gulf Coast Supply	Designer: Carlos M. Segura Jr.
7409	Magna IV	Designer: Micheal Puckett
7410	Acard Printing	Designer: Carlos M. Segura Jr.
7411	Sullivant Rush Cross Realty Inc.	Designer: Micheal Puckett

7411

7412
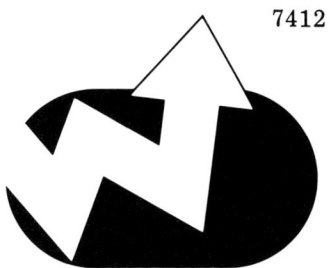

7416
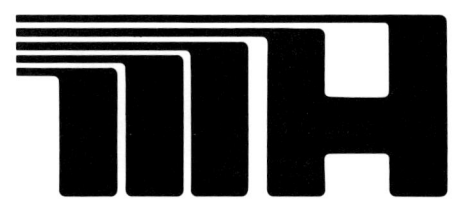

7413

7417
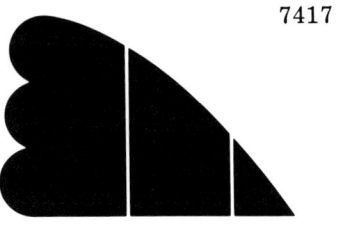

7414

7418
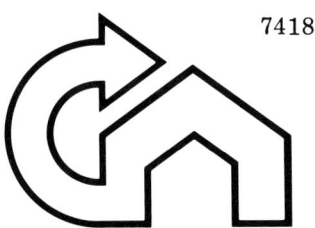

7415

7419

7420

7421

7422

7412	Woodmeyer	Designer: Carlos M. Segura Jr.
7413	Parker Chemicals	Designer: Carlos M. Segura Jr.
7414	Beachside Resorts	Designer: Carlos M. Segura Jr.
7415	Kimm's Trading Company	Designer: Micheal Puckett
7416	Merchandise House	Designer: Carlos M. Segura Jr.
7417	Seabreeze	Designer: Carlos M. Segura Jr.
7418	Group for Solar Energy	Designer: Carlos M. Segura Jr.
7419	George Edmonston Jr. (writer)	Designer: Carlos M. Segura Jr.
7420	Deneal's	Designer: Carlos M. Segura Jr.
7421	Express Repair Service	Designer: Carlos M. Segura Jr.
7422	Purpera & Sons Home Center	Designer: Carlos M. Segura Jr.

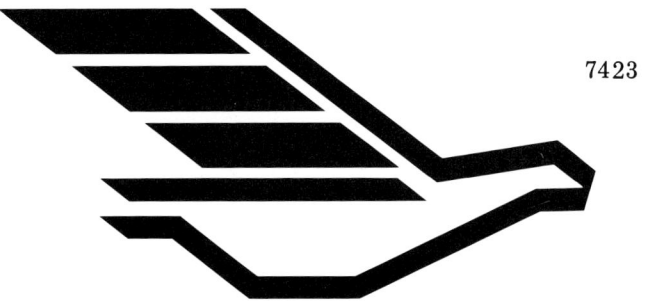

7423

7424

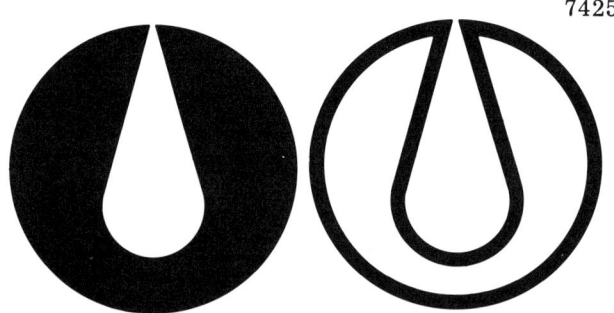

7425

7426

7427

7428

7429

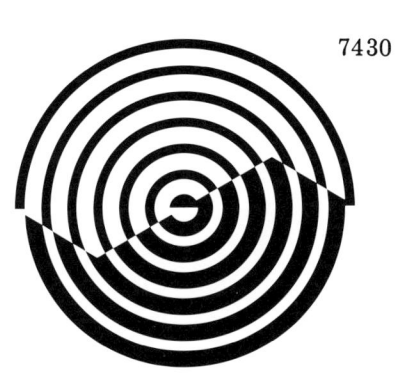

7430

7423	Seagull Communications Designer: Carlos M. Segura Jr.
7424	Blackburn Productions Designer: Winston Taylor
7425	Parkville Water Works Designer: Carlos M. Segura Jr.
7426	John Allphin Designer: Mike Powers
7427	Unigraphics Corporation Designer: Carlos M. Segura Jr.
7428	Dipak, S.A. Designer: Diana Garcia de Tolone
7429	Diana Garcia and Associates Designer: Diana Garcia de Tolone
7430	Impex International Corporation Designer: Diana Garcia de Tolone

7431

7434

7432

7435

7433

distribuidora
Atoto, S.A.

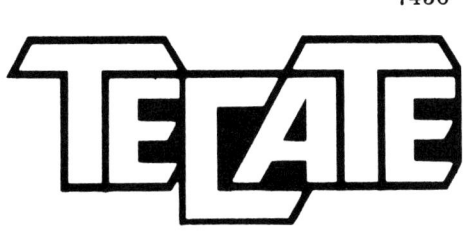

7436

7437

7438

7439

7440

7431	Plasticos Impala, S.A. Designer: Diana Garcia de Tolone	
7432	Cia. Abille, S.A. Designer: Diana Garcia de Tolone	
7433	Distribuidora Atoto, S.A. Designer: Diana Garcia de Tolone	
7434	Associated Engineering Test Laboratories Designer: Allan Miller	
7435	Designer Craftsmen Designer: Allan Miller	
7436	Tecate Designer: Allan Miller	
7437	Acadia Landscaping Designer: Allan Miller	
7438	Baja Inn Hotel Designer: Allan Miller	
7439	Febca Designer: Allan Miller	
7440	Grupo Cinco Designer: Allan Miller	

7441

7445

7442

7446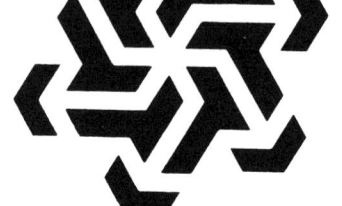

7443

7447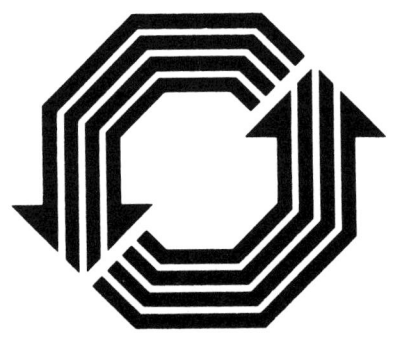

7444

7448

7449

VALUMED

7450

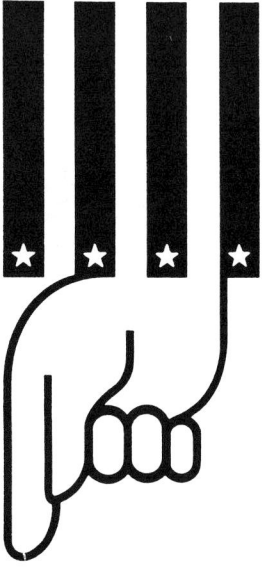

7451

7441	Calafia Consultores	Designer: Allan Miller
7442	Keil Investment Brokers	Designer: Allan Miller
7443	MTC	Designer: Allan Miller
7444	Designcore de Mexico	Designer: Allan Miller
7445	Acapulco Productions	Designer: Allan Miller
7446	Nuevo Centro Urbano	Designer: Allan Miller
7447	Harcourt-Brace-Johanovich	Designer: Allan Miller
7448	Art Council	Designer: Allan Miller
7449	Diostigre	Designer: Allan Miller
7450	Valumed	Designer: Allan Miller
7451	Plaza Camino Real/Mission Valley Center	Designer: Allan Miller

7452

7456

7453

7457

7454

7458

7455
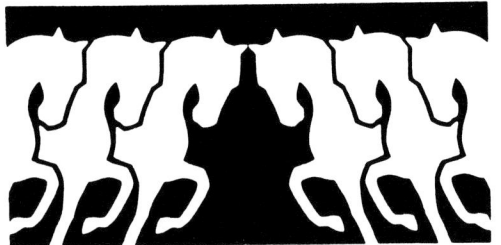

7459

GEROTOURS

7460

7461

7462

7452	Allan Miller & Associates	Designer: Allan Miller
7453	News	Designer: Allan Miller
7454	Restaurante Califia	Designer: Allan Miller
7455	National Horse Show	Designer: Allan Miller
7456	Acapulco Gold Cup Race	Designer: Allan Miller
7457	Martex	Designer: Allan Miller
7458	Servicios Turisticos	Designer: Allan Miller
7459	Jardines de la Mesa	Designer: Allan Miller
7460	Gerotours	Designer: Allan Miller
7461	Agencias Martin Loya	Designer: Allan Miller
7462	Alta Tension	Designer: Allan Miller

7463

7467

7464

7468

7465

7466

PENTA

7469

BORDER WHOLESALE

7470

7471

7472

clamex

7473

7463	Jardines de Chapultepec	Designer: Allan Miller
7464	Solarmex	Designer: Allan Miller
7465	Royale	Designer: Allan Miller
7466	Penta	Designer: Allan Miller
7467	Beauty Supply	Designer: Allan Miller
7468	Costa Palma	Designer: Allan Miller
7469	Desarrollos Arquitecturas Maritimos	Designer: Allan Miller
7470	Border Imports	Designer: Allan Miller
7471	Ponys	Designer: Allan Miller
7472	Potros	Designer: Allan Miller
7473	Clamex	Designer: Allan Miller

7474

7478

7475

7479

7476

7480

7477

7481

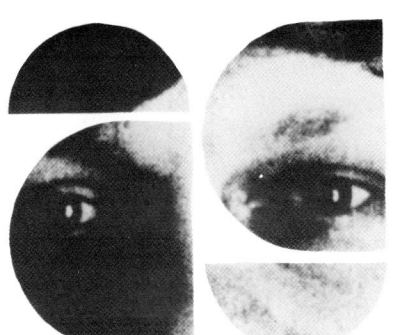

7482

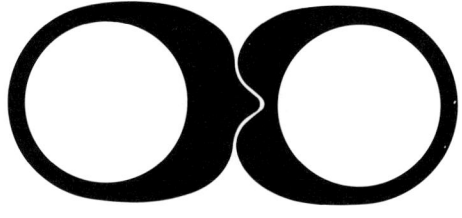

7483

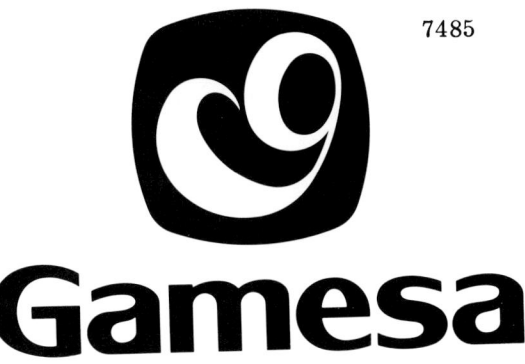

7484

7485

7474	All American Sports Network Designer: Allan Miller	
7475	Sunshine Unlimited Solar Systems Designer: Allan Miller	
7476	Goffstein, Gaston, & Nakash Designer: Allan Miller	
7477	Palomar Legal Services Designer: Allan Miller	
7478	Promont Designer: Allan Miller	
7479	Aerotopomex Designer: Allan Miller	
7480	Roxbury Publishing Co. Designer: Allan Miller	
7481	Laboratorio de Diseno y Analisis de Mercado Designer: Arie J. Geurts	
7482	Arie J. Geurts Designer: Arie J. Geurts	
7483	Mr. & Mrs. Geurts Designer: Arie J. Geurts	
7484	Constanza Geurts Designer: Arie J. Geurts	
7485	Gamesa S. A. Designer: Arie J. Geurts	

7486

7490

7487

7491

7488

7492

7489

7493

7494

7495

7496

7497

7486	American Greeting Corporation	
	Designer: Arthur Congdon & Jack Weller	
	Lippincott & Margulies, Inc.	
7487	Friendly IceCream Corporation	
	Designer: Arthur Congdon & Susuma Harada	
	Lippincott & Margulies, Inc.	
7488	R.H. Johnson Company	
	Designer: Arthur Congdon	
	Congdon Macdonald Inc.	
7489	Movenpik	
	Designer: Arthur Congdon	
	Lippincott & Margulies, Inc.	
7490	Ortho Pharmaceuticals	
	Designer: Arthur Congdon	
	Lippincott & Margulies, Inc.	
7491	Norwalk Montessori Association	
	Designer: Arthur Congdon	
	Congdon Macdonald Inc.	
7492	Fleetwood Enterprises Inc.	
	Designer: Arthur Congdon	
	Lippincott & Margulies, Inc.	
7493	Diners Club International	
	Designer: Arthur Congdon & Bruce Macdonald	
	Congdon Macdonald Inc.	
7494	Leadership Resources Inc.	
	Designer: Arthur Congdon	
	Congdon Macdonald Inc.	
7495	Trinity College	
	Designer: Arthur Congdon	
	Congdon Macdonald Inc.	
7496	Lyon Moving & Storage	
	Designer: Arthur Congdon/Don Ervin/Paul Calle	
7497	Oxbow Ranch	
	Designer: Arthur Congdon	
	Lippincott & Margulies, Inc.	

7498

7502
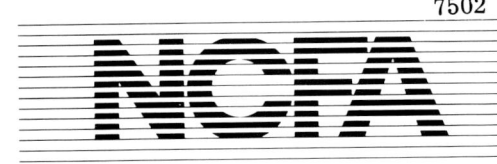

7499

7503

7500

7504

7501

7505

7498	K & B Drugs	
	Designer: Arthur Congdon	
	Lippincott & Margulies, Inc.	
7499	United Van Lines	
	Designer: Arthur Congdon & Michael Toomey	
	Lippincott & Margulies, Inc.	
7500	Harris Teeter Supermarkets	
	Designer: Arthur Congdon	
	Lippincott & Margulies, Inc.	
7501	Pasquale Food Company	
	Designer: Arthur Congdon	
	Lippincott & Margulies, Inc.	
7502	National Consumer Finance Association	
	Designer: Arthur Congdon	
7503	New England Association for Hospital Development	
	Designer: Arthur Congdon	
7504	United States Employment Service U.S. Department of Labor	
	Designer: Arthur Congdon	
7505	Sikorsky	
	Designer: Arthur Congdon	
	Lippincott & Margulies, Inc.	
7506	Private Book Collection	
	Designer: Arthur Congdon	
	Congdon Macdonald Inc.	
7507	Thrushwood Realty	
	Designer: Arthur Congdon	
7508	Volume Shoe Corporation	
	Designer: Arthur Congdon	
	Lippincott & Margulies, Inc.	

7509

7513

7510
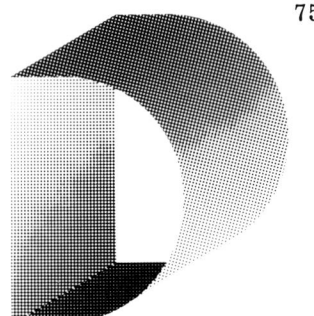

7514

7511

7515

7512

7516

7517

7518

7519

7520

7509 Cassano Enterprises
   Designer: Arthur Congdon
    Lippincott & Margulies, Inc.

7510 Digital Associates
   Designer: Arthur Congdon
    Congdon Macdonald Inc.

7511 The Bank of California
   Designer: Arthur Congdon
    Lippincott & Margulies, Inc.

7512 Southend Development
   Designer: Arthur Congdon

7513 Master Marketing Group
   Designer: Arthur Congdon

7514 Ameritrust
   Designer: Arthur Congdon & Susumu Harada
    Lippincott & Margulies, Inc.

7515 Sports MetaSkills
   Designer: Arthur Congdon
    Congdon Macdonald Inc.

7516 Volume Shoe Corporation
   Designer: Arthur Congdon & Abner Gutierrez
    Lippincott & Margulies, Inc.

7517 The Great Atlantic & Pacific Tea Company
   Designer: Arthur Congdon
    Lippincott & Margulies, Inc.

7518 First Union National Bank
   Designer: Arthur Congdon
    Lippincott & Margulies, Inc.

7519 Carousel
   Designer: Arthur Congdon
    Lippincott & Margulies, Inc.

7520 Volume Shoe Corporation
   Designer: Arthur Congdon
    Lippincott & Margulies, Inc.

7521

7525

7522

7526

7523

7527

7524

7528

7529

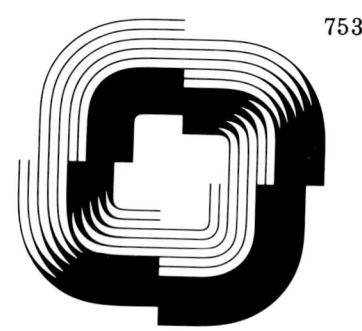

7530

7531

7532

7521   Jonah Inc.
Designer: Arthur Congdon
   Congdon Macdonald Inc.

7522   Mobay Chemical
Designer: Arthur Congdon
   Lippincott & Margulies, Inc.

7523   Melville Shoe
Designer: Arthur Congdon & David Bloch
   Lippincott & Margulies, Inc.

7524   SafeCo Insurance
Designer: Arthur Congdon

7525   Darien Connecticut Indian Guides
Designer: Arthur Congdon
   Congdon Macdonald Inc.

7526   American Bancorp
Designer: Arthur Congdon
   Lippincott & Margulies, Inc.

7527   Arthur Treacher's
Designer: Arthur Congdon & Raphael Boguslav
   Lippincott & Margulies, Inc.

7528   Fidelity Federal Savings and Loan
Designer: Arthur Congdon
   Lippincott & Margulies, Inc.

7529   Melville Shoe
Designer: Arthur Congdon
   Lippincott & Margulies, Inc.

7530   The Investment Properties Group
Designer: Arthur Congdon
   Congdon Macdonald Inc.

7531   Budget Rent - a - Car
Designer: Arthur Congdon

7532   Ladrillera Monterrey S.A.
Designer: Arthur Congdon
   Lippincott & Margulies, Inc.

7533

7537

7534

7538

7535

7539

7536

7540

7541

7542

7543

7544

7533	Cementos Tolteca	Designer: Arie J. Geurts
7534	Servicios Profesionales	Designer: Arie J. Geurts
7535	Carsa	Designer: Arie J. Geurts
7536	Preconcreto	Designer: Arie J. Geurts
7537	Premesa	Designer: Arie J. Geurts
7538	Sacsa	Designer: Arie J. Geurts
7539	Cemento Campana	Designer: Arie J. Geurts
7540	Cemento Victoria	Designer: Arie J. Geurts
7541	Cemento Atoyac	Designer: Arie J. Geurts
7542	Cemento Centenario	Designer: Arie J. Geurts
7543	Transmar	Designer: Arie J. Geurts
7544	Procalsa	Designer: Arie J. Geurts

7545

7549

7546

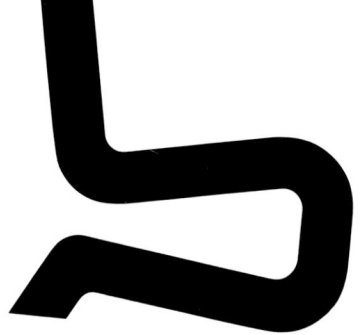

7550

7547

7551

7548

7552

7553

7554

7545	Codi	Designer: Arie J. Geurts
7546	Buck	Designer: Arie J. Geurts
7547	NOVUM Gebrauchsgrafik	Designer: Arie J. Geurts
7548	United, financial institution	Designer: Arie J. Geurts
7549	Ignacio Villareal	Designer: Arie J. Geurts
7550	Dispersion S.A.	Designer: Arie J. Geurts
7551	United, financial institution	Designer: Arie J. Geurts
7552	Emyco S.A.	Designer: Arie J. Geurts
7553	Radio station project	Designer: Arie J. Geurts
7554	Radio station project	Designer: Arie J. Geurts

7555

7559

7556

7560

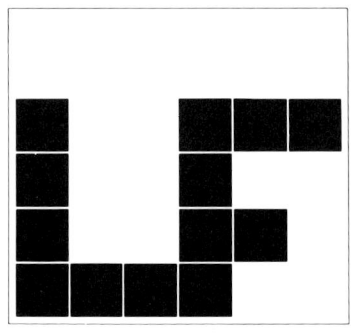
7557

7561

7558

7562

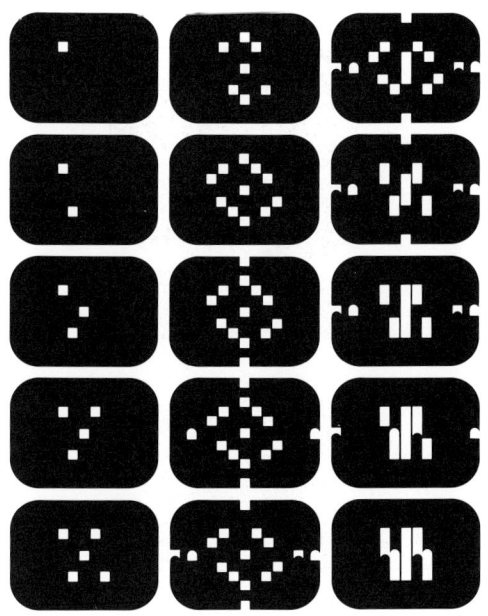

7563

7564

7555	Spectra-Media Communications	Designer: Arie J. Geurts
7556	Productos Sahler	Designer: Arie J. Geurts
7557	L. Fernandez	Designer: Arie J. Geurts
7558	Lance S.A.	Designer: Arie J. Geurts
7559	Langeman & Cape	Designer: Arie J. Geurts
7560	Clarion car radios	Designer: Arie J. Geurts
7561	Carnabi	Designer: Arie J. Geurts
7562	DOD	Designer: Arie J. Geurts
7563	Hunt, Leuchars, & Hepburn Ltd.	Designer: Arie J. Geurts
7564	Spies	Designer: Arie J. Geurts
7565	S.A. Railways	Designer: Arie J. Geurts

7565

7566

7570

7567

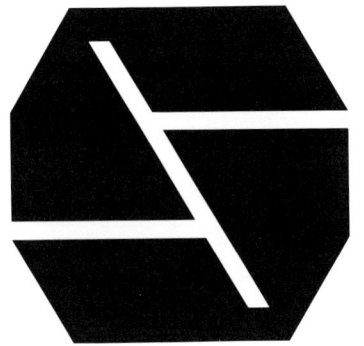
7571

7568

7572

7569

7573

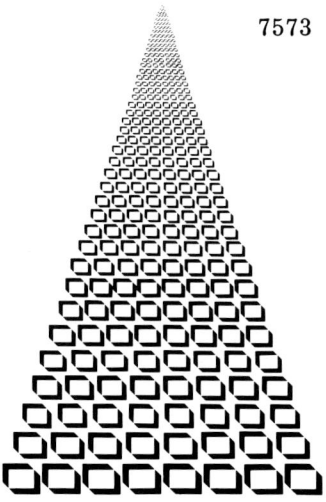

7574

7575

7566	"Conmaeca" Designer: Arie J. Geurts & Mucio Contreras
7567	Construction Company Designer: Arie J. Geurts
7568	R.F. Tophovan Designer: Arie J. Geurts
7569	Mexican Paper/Cellulose Seminar Designer: Arie J. Geurts
7570	Jewish Sports Club, Mexico Designer: Arie J. Geurts
7571	Safrex tools Designer: Arie J. Geurts
7572	Palm Designer: Arie J. Geurts
7573	Carton y Papel ole Mexico S.A. Designer: Arie J. Geurts
7574	Henred Trailers Designer: Arie J. Geurts
7575	Larry Alexander Advertising Designer: Arie J. Geurts

7576

7579

7577

7580

7578

7581

7576	CPM Designer: Arie J. Geurts & Mucio Contreras
7577	Ignacio Villareal Designer: Arie J. Geurts
7578	Profamilia S.A. Designer: Graham Edwards
7579	Employment development Designer: Graham Edwards
7580	Man & Universe Designer: Graham Edwards
7581	Orduno, employment service Designer: Graham Edwards
7582	Industrializadora de cacao de Tabasco S.A. Designer: Graham Edwards
7583	Coleccion Marke Designer: Graham Edwards
7584	La Campana S.A. Designer: Graham Edwards

7585

agpa

7589

JANET

7586

iMEF

7590

RODEX

7587

cnis

7591

Chambrulé

7588

infratur

7592

super3

7593

7594

7595

7585	Carton y Papel de Mexico S.A. Designer: Graham Edwards
7586	Mexican Institute of Finance Executives Designer: Graham Edwards
7587	Mexican Paper Association Designer: Graham Edwards
7588	Tourist development Designer: Graham Edwards
7589	Janet, toy manufacturers Designer: Graham Edwards
7590	Rodex S.A. Designer: Graham Edwards
7591	Cavas Bach S.A. Designer: Graham Edwards
7592	Kellogs de Mexico S.A. Designer: Graham Edwards
7593	Muebles Norden S.A. Designer: Graham Edwards
7594	Parera S.A. Designer: Graham Edwards
7595	Balseca S.A. Designer: Graham Edwards

7596

7600

7597

7601

7598

7602

7599

7603

7604

7605

7596	U.S. Sanitary	Designer: Graham Edwards
7597	Institute for Advanced Studies	Designer: Graham Edwards
7598	Productos Congelados S.A.	Designer: Graham Edwards
7599	Comercial Mexicana S.A.	Designer: Graham Edwards
7600	Balseca	Designer: Graham Edwards
7601	Wilson S.A.	Designer: Graham Edwards
7602	Incataba	Designer: Graham Edwards
7603	Chiclet Adams de Mexico S.A.	Designer: Graham Edwards
7604	Ebesa	Designer: Graham Edwards
7605	Cigarrera la Moderna	Designer: Graham Edwards
7606	Panam S.A.	Designer: Graham Edwards

7606

7607

7610

7608

7611

7609

7612

7613

7614

7615

7607	Campbells de Mexico S.A.	Designer: Graham Edwards
7608	Industrial de Alimentos	Designer: Graham Edwards
7609	Ice Cream Parlor	Designer: Graham Edwards
7610	Ricardo's Mexican Restaurant	Designer: Graham Edwards
7611	Cereales Industrializados S.A.	Designer: Graham Edwards
7612	Ornelas S.A.	Designer: Graham Edwards
7613	Boutique Vicky	Designer: Graham Edwards
7614	San Jemo	Designer: Graham Edwards
7615	Christmas Theme CPM	Designer: Graham Edwards

7616

7619

7617

7620

7618

7621

7622

7623

7624

7625

7616	International aerosol seminar Designer: Graham Edwards
7617	Ebesa Designer: Graham Edwards
7618	Las Conchas Designer: Graham Edwards
7619	Tourist development Designer: Graham Edwards
7620	Boutique Arlequin Designer: Graham Edwards
7621	Ricardo's Mexican Restaurant Designer: Graham Edwards
7622	Aires del Mayab Designer: Victor Sanjuan
7623	Carton y Papel de Mexico S.A. Designer: Victor Sanjuan & Alex Honda
7624	Christmas Theme CPM Designer: Victor Sanjuan
7625	Carton y Papel de Mexico S.A. Designer: Victor Sanjuan

7626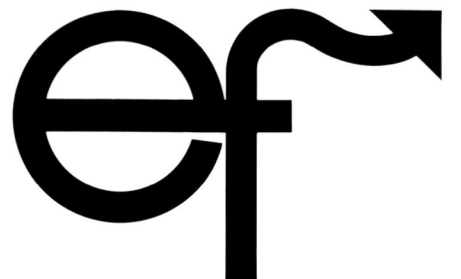

7629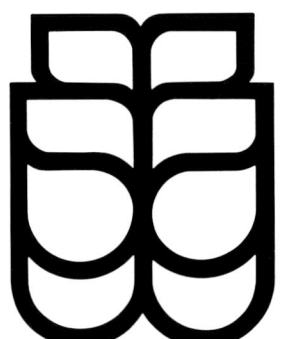

7627

7630

7631

7628

7632

7633

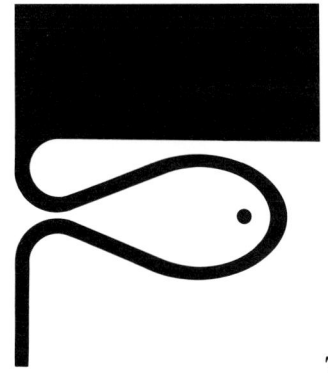

7634

7635

7626	Mexican Finance Executives Association Designer: Victor Sanjuan
7627	Christmas Theme CPM Designer: Victor Sanjuan
7628	Mexico City sports promotion Designer: Luis E. Ramirez
7629	Mexican Ministry of Agriculture Designer: Luis E. Ramirez
7630	Mexican Ministry of Finance Designer: Luis E. Ramirez
7631	Administrative Studies Designer: Luis E. Ramirez
7632	Grupo Castell S.A. Designer: Luis E. Ramirez
7633	Andres Garcia Designer: Andres Garcia
7634	Banco Rural de Pesca Designer: Andres Garcia
7635	Collegio de Bachilleres Designer: Andres Garcia

7636

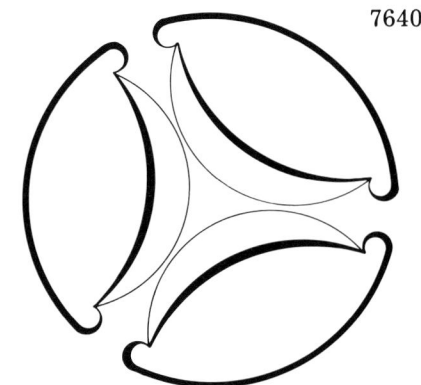
7640

7637

7641

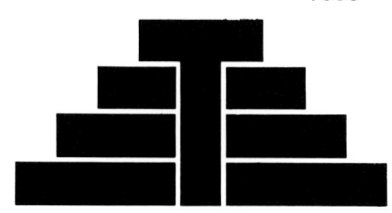
7638

7639

7642

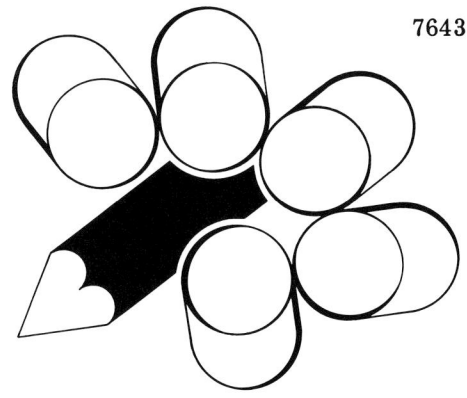

7643

7644

7645

7636 "Root"
Designer: Andres Garcia

7637 College for architects
Designer: Andres Garcia

7638 Mexican Tourism Theme
Designer: Andres Garcia

7639 Agriculture/Cattle Association
Designer: Andres Garcia

7640 Mexican Association of Bakers
Designer: Fay Medina

7641 Arcuitur S.C.
Designer: Fay Medina

7642 Duraclean S.A.
Designer: Fay Medina

7643 Theme for design siminar (Mexico)
Designer: Fay Medina

7644 ICSID, XI Congres of industrial design, Mexico
Designer: Fay Medina

7645 Africa S.A.
Designer: Fay Medina

7646

7649

7650

7647

7651

7648

7652

7653

7654

7655

7656

7646 Fermex S.A.
Designer: Fay Medina

7647 State of Mexico, archives
Designer: Fay Medina

7648 State of Mexico, waiting room
Designer: Fay Medina

7649 State of Mexico, reception
Designer: Fay Medina

7650 State of Mexico, board room
Designer: Fay Medina

7651 State of Mexico, planning
Designer: Fay Medina

7652 State of Mexico, cleaning
Designer: Fay Medina

7653 Display International S.A.
Designer: Luis E. Ramirez

7654 Creativity and Design
Designer: Luis E. Ramirez & Sergio Colin

7655 Sears Roebuck de Mexico S.A.
Designer: Luis E. Ramirez

7656 S.H.C.P.
Designer: Luis E. Ramirez

7657

7661

7658

7662

aristos

7659

7663

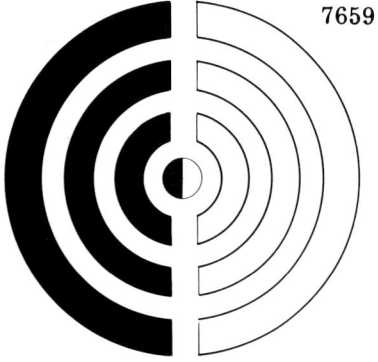

7660

7664

7665

7666

7657	Seminar for secretaries Designer: Luis E. Ramirez
7658	Mexican Ministry of Finance Designer: Luis E. Ramirez
7659	Audio Electronica de Mexico S.A. Designer: Luis E. Ramirez
7660	Luis Olvera, designer Designer: Luis Olvera
7661	Aurioles y Associates Designer: Luis Olvera
7662	Aristos S.A. Designer: Luis Olvera
7663	Casa Rosos S.A. Designer: Fco. Gutierrez
7664	Mexican Citrus Growers Association Designer: Fco. Gutierrez
7665	Mexican Lemon Growers Association Designer: Fco. Gutierrez
7666	Bowling Club CPM Designer: Fco. Gutierrez

7667

7668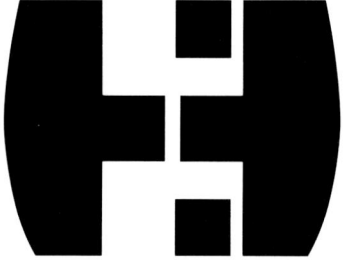

7669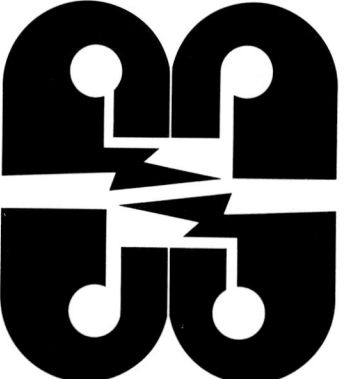

7670

7671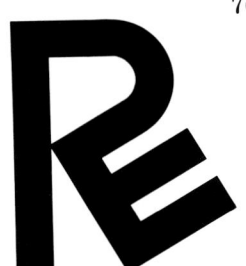

7672

7673

7674

(Cupid - Eat your Heart Out)

7675

7676

7667   Paper and Cellulose Association
Designer: Fco. Gutierrez

7668   Electrica Hernandez
Designer: Fco. Gutierrez

7669   Electrica Montevideo
Designer: Fco. Gutierrez

7670   Cal Cru
Designer: Elaine M. Lyerly

7671   Rimsky Enterprises, Inc.
Designer: Elaine M. Lyerly

7672   Ramada Inn-Coliseum
Designer: Elaine M. Lyerly

7673   Dr. Linda C. Gardner
Designer: Elaine M. Lyerly

7674   Eve Communication Service, Inc.
Designer: Elaine M. Lyerly

7675   Landscape Design
Designer: Elaine M. Lyerly

7676   Khaki's
Designer: Elaine M. Lyerly

7677

7678

7679

7680

7681

7682

7683

LIBRARY

7684

7685

Ratterree Company

7686

HUCKLEBERRY DEN

7677	Moore Electric Supply, Inc.	
	Designer: Elaine M. Lyerly	
7678	Ramada Inn-Coliseum	
	Designer: Elaine M. Lyerly	
7679	Ramada Inn-Coliseum	
	Designer: Elaine M. Lyerly	
7680	Monroe Enquirer Journal	
	Designer: Elaine M. Lyerly	
7681	Rockhill Concert Ballet Co.	
	Designer: Elaine M. Lyerly	
7682	Equity, Inc.	
	Designer: Elaine M. Lyerly	
7683	Ramada Inn-Coliseum	
	Designer: Elaine M. Lyerly	
7684	Market Data Associates	
	Designer: Elaine M. Lyerly	
7685	Ratterree Knife Company, Inc.	
	Designer: Elaine M. Lyerly & Diane W. Lay	
7686	Ramada Inn-Coliseum	
	Designer: Elaine M. Lyerly	

7687

7691

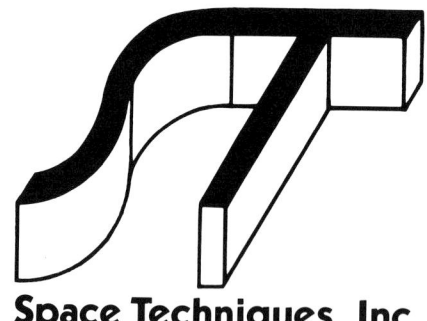

7688

7692

7689

7693

7690

7694

7695 Twin Anchors Marina

7696 The Spencer Group

7697 Interior Design by Stefano

7698 Catholic Charity Committee

7687	Edwin M. Rollins, Inc.	Designer: Diane W. Lay
7688	Space Techniques, Inc.	Designer: Diane W. Lay
7689	G.M. Hogshead Co.	Designer: Diane W. Lay
7690	Morris & Associates Realtors	Designer: Diane W. Lay
7691	Florence Crittenton Services	Designer: Karen Chambers
7692	Mammouth Mountain Lodge	Designer: Douglas Wilson
7693	Fleetwood Cartage	Designer: Douglas Wilson
7694	Paradise Found	Designer: Douglas Wilson
7695	Twin Anchors Marine	Designer: Douglas Wilson
7696	The Spencer Group	Designer: Douglas Wilson
7697	Interior Design	Designer: Douglas Wilson
7698	Catholic Charity Committee	Designer: Douglas Wilson

7699

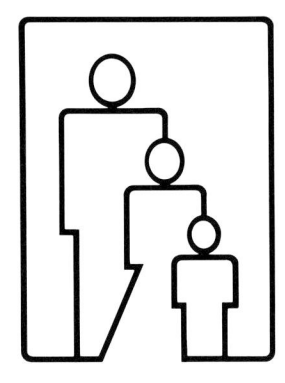
Family Counseling Center

7703

7700

7704

The Lincoln Theater

7701

7702

7705

Nevada Balloon Club

7706

7707

7708

7699	Family Counseling Center	Designer: Douglas Wilson
7700	Len Bannister Advertising	Designer: Douglas Wilson
7701	Sun Ray Products, Inc.	Designer: Douglas Wilson
7702	Gillmore & Right Co.	Designer: Douglas Wilson
7703	Boats Inn	Designer: Douglas Wilson
7704	The Lincoln Theater	Designer: Douglas Wilson
7705	Nevada Balloon Club	Designer: Douglas Wilson
7706	Eagle Mobile Homes & Campers	Designer: Douglas Wilson
7707	Rochester Steel	Designer: Douglas Wilson
7708	Dixie 5	Designer: Douglas Wilson

7709

aids

7710

7711

7712

7713

7714

7715

7709	Allen Industrial Development Statistics Designer: Douglas Wilson
7710	Bumble + Bumble Hair Salon Designer: Mike Quon
7711	Metropolitan Transit Authority Designer: Mike Quon & Ed Flanagan
7712	Ski Togs Sportswear Designer: Mike Quon
7713	Paracom, Inc. Designer: Mike Quon
7714	World Invitational Tournament Designer: Mike Quon
7715	Uptown Eddie's Restaurant Designer: Hart Communications, Inc.

7716

7720

7717

7721

7718

7722

7719

7723

7724

7725

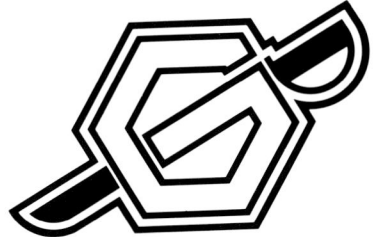

7726

7727

7716	The Royal Axman, Inc. Designer: Hart Communications, Inc.
7717	Second Cousin Restaurant Designer: Hart Communications, Inc.
7718	Agriculture & Energy Designer: Hart Communications, Inc.
7719	Harmony Classic, Inc. Designer: Hart Communications, Inc.
7720	Smith-Scharff Designer: Hart Communications, Inc.
7721	Avondale Swim & Tennis Club Designer: Don Connelly & Associates
7722	The Breakers Designer: Don Connelly & Associates
7723	Specialty Graphics Designer: Don Connelly & Associates
7724	The Palms Designer: Don Connelly & Associates
7725	Associated Rubber Designer: Don Connelly & Associates
7726	Georgia General Soccer (proposal) Designer: Don Connelly & Associates
7727	Video Record Services Designer: Don Connelly & Associates

7728

7732
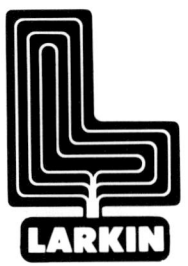

7729

7733

7730

7734

7731

7735

7736

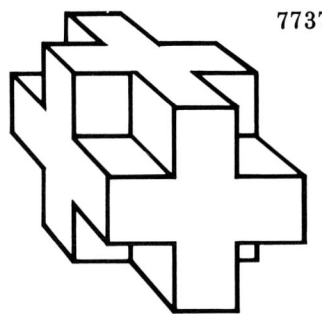

7737

7738

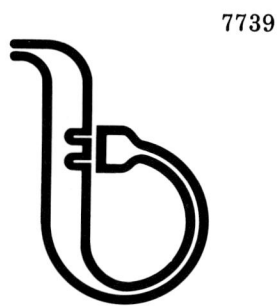

7739

7728	National Graphics Designer: Don Connelly & Associates
7729	The Country Store Designer: Don Connelly & Associates
7730	The Sails Designer: Don Connelly & Associates
7731	Sunbelt Designer: Don Connelly & Associates
7732	Larkin Coils Designer: Don Connelly & Associates
7733	Holder Well Company Designer: Don Connelly & Associates
7734	Bullard Realty Designer: Don Connelly & Associates
7735	Moores Department Store (proposal) Designer: Don Connelly & Associates
7736	Bettys Tours Designer: Don Connelly & Associates
7737	Red Cross-Metro Atlanta Designer: Don Connelly & Associates
7738	Organizational Services Inc. Designer: Don Connelly & Associates
7739	Bryant Electronics Designer: Don Connelly & Associates

7740

7744

7741

7745

7742
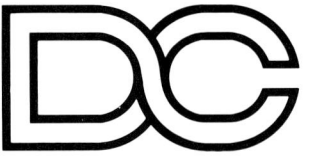

7746
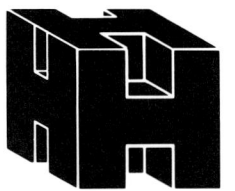

7743

7747

7748

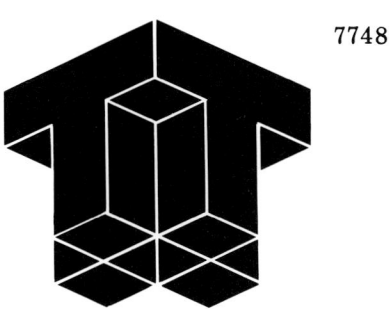

7749

7750

7751

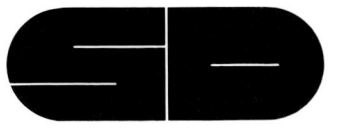

7740	Chaney & Associates	
	Designer: Don Connelly & Associates	
7741	Crusader Equipment Inc.	
	Designer: Don Connelly & Associates	
7742	Don Connelly	
	Designer: Don Connelly & Associates	
7743	Modular Movers	
	Designer: Don Connelly & Associates	
7744	Reynolds Asphalt Paving	
	Designer: Don Connelly & Associates	
7745	Reconstruction Inc.	
	Designer: Don Connelly & Associates	
7746	Hirt Realty	
	Designer: Don Connelly & Associates	
7747	Arthritus Foundation (proposal)	
	Designer: Don Connelly & Associates	
7748	Trust Conference	
	Designer: Don Connelly & Associates	
7749	Practitioners Forum	
	Designer: Don Connelly & Associates	
7750	Metrocraft Publishing	
	Designer: Don Connelly & Associates	
7751	Stanley Drugs	
	Designer: Don Connelly & Associates	

7752

7756

7753

7757

7754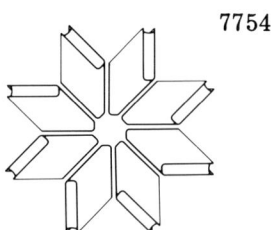

7758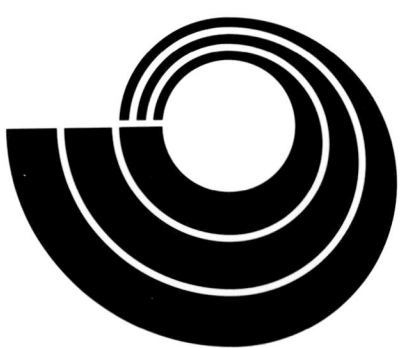

7755

7759

7760

CHAUMONT
In Cherry Hills

7761

7762

7752	Journal of Reading	
	Designer: Don Connelly & Associates	
7753	Georgia Heart Association "Lifeline"	
	Designer: Don Connelly & Associates	
7754	Georgia Bankers Association	
	Designer: Don Connelly & Associates	
7755	New Market Business Park	
	Designer: Don Connelly & Associates	
7756	Roxborough Park Development Corporation	
	Designer: Arvid Wallen & Duane Wiens	
7757	Carlson, Inc.	
	Designer: Carl Baden & Duane Wiens	
7758	Luby Enterprises	
	Designer: Carl Baden & Arvid Wallen	
7759	Tana Corporation	
	Designer: Carl Baden & Duane Wiens	
7760	Barton Investments, Inc.	
	Designer: Arvid Wallen & Carl Baden	
7761	Matthews Real Estate Company	
	Designer: Arvid Wallen & Carl Baden	
7762	Viewpoint Associates	
	Designer: Carl Baden & Duane Wiens	

BARCLAY TOWERS

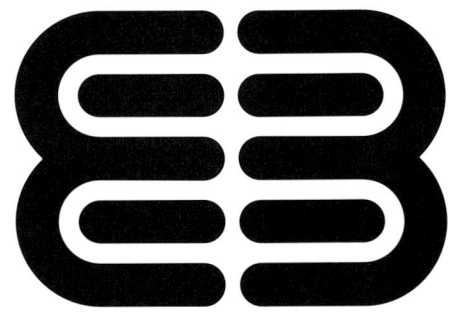

7770

7771

7763	Aurora Plaza Hotel Designer: Carl Baden & Duane Wiens
7764	Western Crude Oil, Inc. Designer: Arvid Wallen & Duane Wiens
7765	Barton Investments, Inc. Designer: Carl Baden & Duane Wiens
7766	Barton Investments, Inc. Designer: Arvid Wallen & Carl Baden
7767	Barclay Towers Designer: Arvid Wallen & Carl Baden
7768	State of Colorado Litter Control Program Designer: Arvid Wallen & Duane Wiens
7769	Wicker Works Video Productions Designer: Tim Kridel & Arvid Wallen
7770	Plan West Designer: Arvid Wallen & Duane Wiens
7771	Agriculture Production Technology, LTD. Designer: Carl Baden & Arvid Wallen
7772	Rockwell International, North American Space Operations Employee Action Circle Designer: Don L. Sterrenburg

7772

7773

7776

7774

7777

7775

7778

7779

7780

7781

7782

7773	Bonin Realty Designer: Don L. Sterrenburg
7774	Practical Sciences, Inc. Designer: Don L. Sterrenburg
7775	Whittier Hills Baptist Church Designer: Don L. Sterrenburg
7776	Interface Educational Consultants Designer: Don L. Sterrenburg
7777	Yankee Sawyer Designer: Don L. Sterrenburg
7778	Universidad Femenina de Mexico Designer: Jose A. Garcia-Luna
7779	Atalaya, international meeting of intellectuals Designer: Jose A. Garcia-Luna
7780	Auto Control Designer: Jose A. Garcia-Luna
7781	Protor (suggested) Designer: Jose A. Garcia-Luna
7782	Estilo Designer: Jose A. Garcia-Luna

7783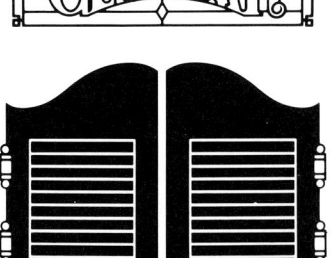

7787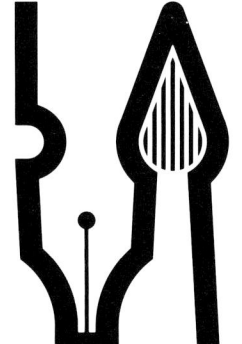

7784

7788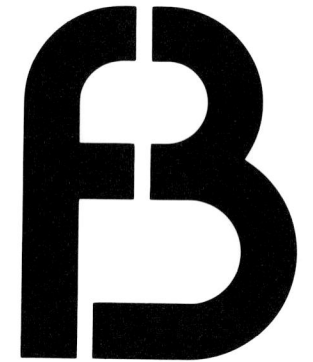

7785

7786

7789

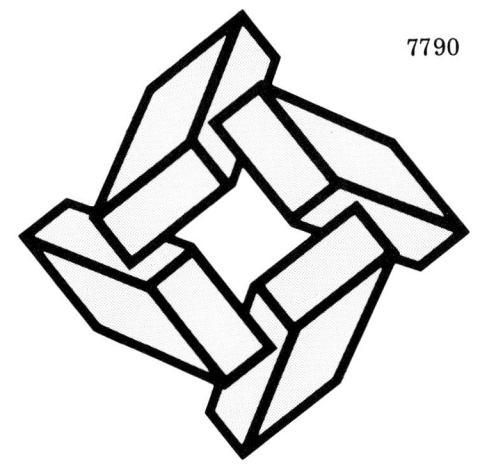

7790

7791

7792

7783	GLCS Bar Designer: Jose A. Garcia-Luna
7784	Encuentro Designer: Jose A. Garcia-Luna
7785	Fundacion Mexicana Para El Desarrollo Rural Designer: Jose A. Garcia-Luna
7786	Banco Aboumrad (suggested) Designer: Jose A. Garcia-Luna
7787	Graphis Designer: Jose A. Garcia-Luna
7788	Jose Garcia-Luna Designer: Jose A. Garcia-Luna
7789	Fernando Bustos, trusteeship Designer: Jose A. Garcia-Luna
7790	Construis Designer: Jose A. Garcia-Luna
7791	Flor Designer: Jose A. Garcia-Luna
7792	The Skin Cancer Foundation Designer: Arthur Eckstein

7799

7793	Dusal Instrument Corp. Designer: Arthur Eckstein
7794	Corporate Programming Inc. Designer: Arthur Eckstein
7795	Struthers Electronics Corp. Designer: Arthur Eckstein
7796	Ibex Pension Actuaries Inc. Designer: Arthur Eckstein
7797	Univac Div. of Sperry Rand Designer: Arthur Eckstein
7798	American ORT Federation Designer: Arthur Eckstein
7799	Paul Kagan Associates, Inc. Designer: Arthur Eckstein
7800	Typographic Images Inc. Designer: Arthur Eckstein
7801	Tri-Seal International Inc. Designer: Arthur Eckstein

7802 AMERICAN SCALE

7805

7803

7806

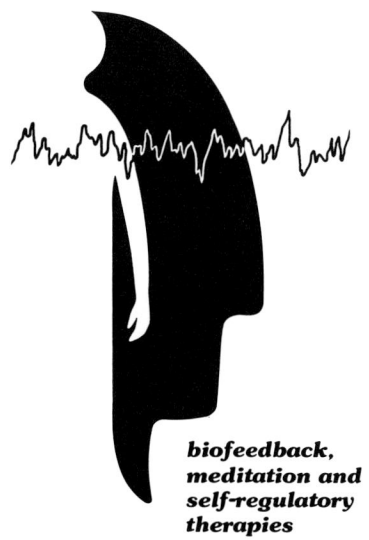

7804

biofeedback, meditation and self-regulatory therapies

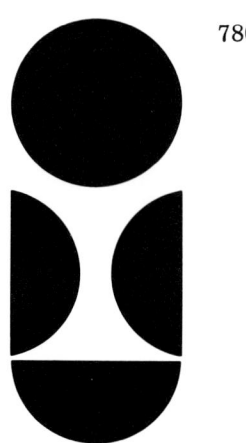

7807

7808

7809

7810

7811

7802	American Scale Corporation Designer: Arthur Eckstein	
7803	Paul Kagan Associates, Inc. Designer: Arthur Eckstein	
7804	Institute for the Study of Human Knowledge, Inc. Designer: Arthur Eckstein	
7805	Studio Film & Tape Inc. Designer: Arthur Eckstein	
7806	National Institute for the Psychotherapies, Inc. Designer: Arhtur Eckstein	
7807	Imco Precision Products Inc. Designer: Arthur Eckstein	
7808	Daryl Cushenbery (personal logo) Designer: Daryl Cushenbery	
7809	Stormont-Vail Regional Medical Center Designer: Daryl Cushenbery	
7810	Florasia (rock group) Designer: Daryl Cushenbery	
7811- 7814	Brock Hotel Corporation Designer: Daryl Cushenbery	

7812

7816

7813

7817

7814

7818

7815

7819

7820

7821

7822

7815	Brock Hotel Corporation Designer: Cindy Maude
7816	Security Benefit Group of Companies Designer: Wanda Prus
7817- 7819	Brock Hotel Corporation Designer: Su Deiter
7820	K-Sweet Radio Designer: Su Deiter
7821	Brock Hotel Corporation Designer: Su Deiter
7822	Brock Hotel Corporation Designer: Su Deiter
7823	Emerson/Nichols/Bailey Designer: Su Deiter

7823

7824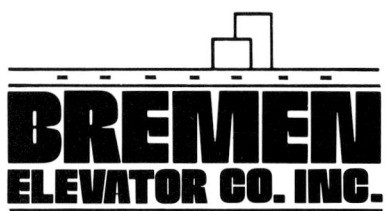

7828

7825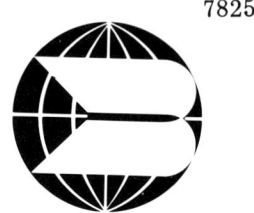

7829

7826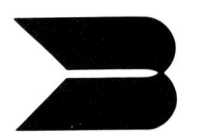

7830

7827

7831

7832

7833

7824   Bremen Elevator Co., Inc.
        Designer: Su Deiter

7825   Brock Real Estate Investment
        Corporation
        Designer: Lynn M. Scannell

7826-
7835   Brock Hotel Corporation
        Designer: Lynn M. Scannell

7834

7835

7836 LEEANN BROOK DESIGN

7840

7837 ALCO
ALCOHOL ENERGY COMPANY

7841

7838 National Hotel
ESTABLISHED 1852
NEVADA CITY, CALIFORNIA

7842

7839

7843

7844

7845

7846

7836	LeeAnn Brook Design Designer: LeeAnn Brook	
7837	Alcohol Energy Company Designer: LeeAnn Brook	
7838	National Hotel Designer: LeeAnn Brook	
7839	Bear Development Corporation Designer: LeeAnn Brook	
7840	Nevada County Aviation Designer: LeeAnn Brook	
7841	Foothill Solar Exchange Designer: LeeAnn Brook	
7842	Nevada County Legal Assistance, Inc. Designer: LeeAnn Brook	
7843	Nevada County Arts Council Designer: LeeAnn Brook	
7844	Astral Glass Designer: LeeAnn Brook	
7845	Sierra Water Systems Designer: LeeAnn Brook	
7846	The Jean Store Designer: LeeAnn Brook	

7847

7851

7848

7852

7849

7853

7854

7850

7855

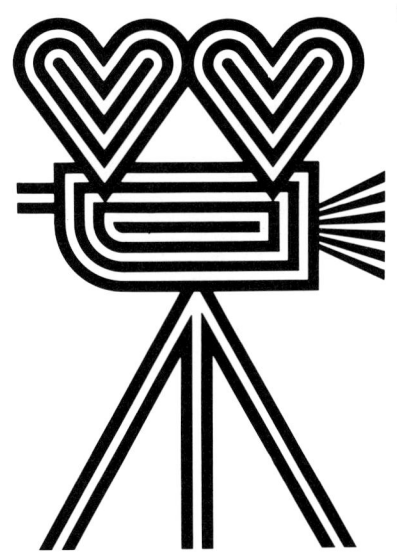

7856

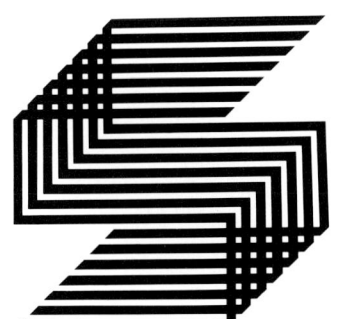

7857

7847	Sierra Timberline Designer: LeeAnn Brook
7848	Erwin Schwarz Jeweler Designer: LeeAnn Brook
7849	J. L. Owens & Company Designer: LeeAnn Brook
7850	Suntech Construction Designer: LeeAnn Brook
7851	Mountain Wool & Weaving Supply Company Designer: LeeAnn Brook
7852	The Magic Carpet Designer: LeeAnn Brook
7853	III Salon de Escultura y Obra Grafica Designer: Jorge Sposari
7854	Guia Civil Qi Designer: Jorge Sposari
7855	La Pelicula Designer: Jorge Sposari
7856	Soifer, Cristales Templados Designer: Jorge Sposari
7857	Primer Concurso Nacional de Diseno y Fabricacion de Mobiliario de Interes Socail Designer: Jorge Sposari

7858

7862

7859

7863

7860

7861

7864

7865

7866

7867

7858	Complejo Habitacional "Bristol Center" Designer: Jorge Sposari
7859	Canas y Flores Producciones Designer: Jorge Sposari
7860	Centro de Arte Fic Designer: Jorge Sposari
7861	Materias Primas Monterrey S.A. Designer: Jorge Sposari
7862	Ernesto Coco Transportes Designer: Jorge Sposari
7863	Producciones del Plata Designer: Jorge Sposari
7864	Econafta Designer: Jorge Sposari
7865	Solector Designer: Jorge Sposari
7866	Accion Cultural y Asistencial Designer: Jorge Sposari
7867	Argentina de Comercio Designer: Jorge Sposari

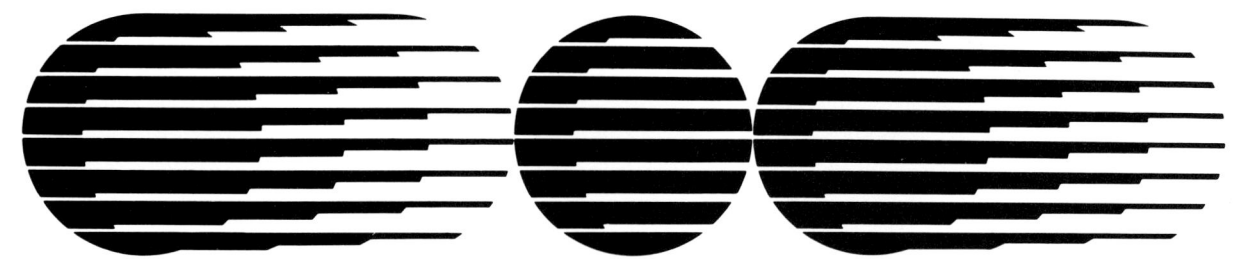

7868

7869

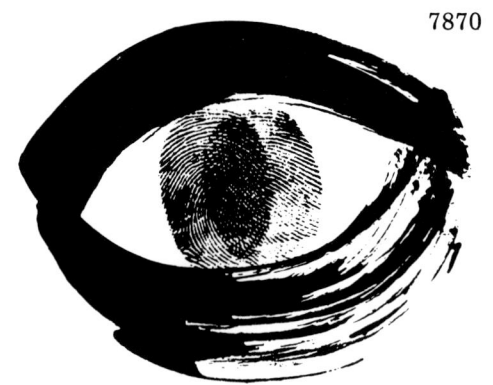

7870

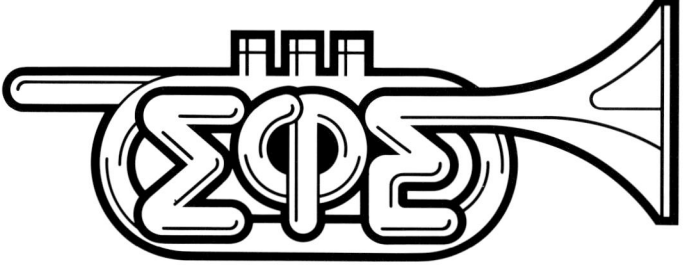

7871

7868	Tecnofon Comunicaciones Designer: Jorge Sposari
7869	Logotipo de la Obra de Teatro: "Woyzeck" Designer: Jorge Sposari
7870	Editorial Grijalbo: Simbolo de la Portada "Los Sentidos Al Aire" Designer: Jorge Sposari
7871	Sigma Phi Epsilon National Fraternity Designer: Michael B. Leidel
7872	Goodies by Gourmet Designer: Patrick Austin
7873	Love & Dugger Designer: George Ybarra & Patrick Austin
7874	Rosenstein's Jewels Designer: Patrick Austin
7875	San Jan Pools, Inc. Designer: George Ybarra & Patrick Austin

7884

7885

7886

7887

7876	CSC Properties	Designer: Patrick Austin
7877	SpectraVision	Designer: George Ybarra & Patrick Austin
7878	Marlene Glasser Public Relations & Advertising	Designer: George Ybarra & Patrick Austin
7879	Barshop Enterprises	Designer: Patrick Austin
7880	Bub Shannon/photography	Designer: Patrick Austin
7881	Advance Signage	Designer: George Ybarra & Patrick Austin
7882	The CFC Group	Designer: Partick Austin
7883	First National Bank of Yorktown	Designer: Patrick Austin & George Ybarra
7884	The Lodge Apartments	Designer: Patrick Austin & George Ybarra
7885	Whispering Oaks Apartments	Designer: Patrick Austin & George Ybarra
7886	Hallenberger & Associates Consulting Engineers	Designer: Partick Austin & George Ybarra
7887	Encinitos Office Building	Designer: Ann Fischer & Patrick Austin

7888

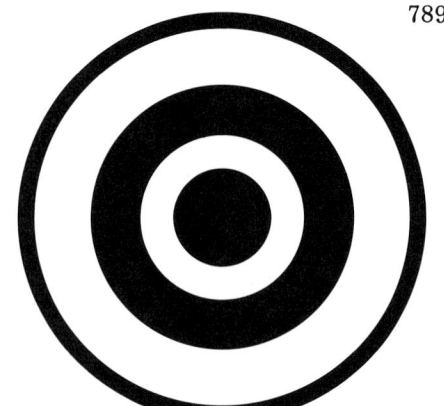

7890

7889

7891

7892

7893

7894

7895

7888	Mini Mail Boxes	Designer: Ann Fischer
7889	Windsor Plaza Shopping Center	Designer: George Ybarra & Patrick Austin
7890	KGRC Radio Station	Designer: Randall R. Roth
7891	Discount King	Designer: Randall R. Roth
7892	Huebner & Henneberg, Architects	Designer: Randall R. Roth
7893	Paintwell Co.	Designer: Randall R. Roth
7894	Hospice of Schenectady	Designer: John DeSieno
7895	Time Center Jewelers	Designer: John DeSieno

7896

7900

7897

7901

7898

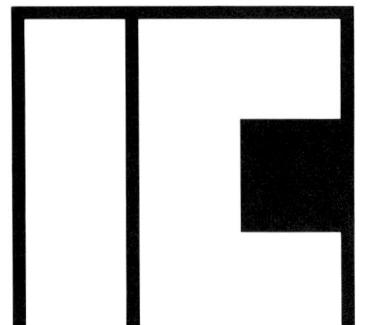

7902

7899

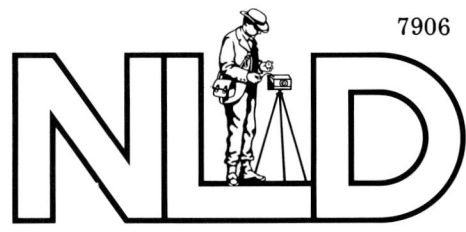

7896	Empire State Convention Center	Designer: John DeSieno
7897–7899	Suburbon Electronics	Designer: Reginald K. Litten
7900	Manifattura Naj-Oleari	Designer: Angelo Sganzerla
7901	Associazione Industriali Varese	Designer: Angelo Sganzerla
7902	Interchoice Contracting	Designer: Angelo Sganzerla
7903	Multi-Press	Designer: Angelo Sganzerla
7904	Honey s. r. l.	Designer: Angelo Sganzerla
7905	Communicateurs Associes	Designer: Angelo Sganzerla
7906	Nino Lo Duca	Designer: Angelo Sganzerla

7915

BECHET'S

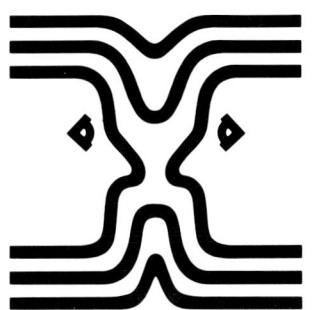

7916

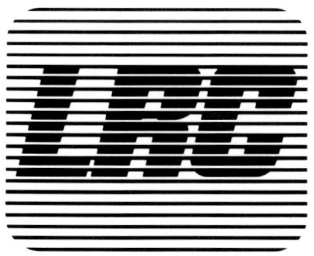

Learning Resource Center

7917

7918

7907	l'Erbolario Designer: Angelo Sganzerla
7908	l'Erbolario Designer: Angelo Sganzerla
7909	Multhipla Designer: Angelo Sganzerla
7910	Galleria Arte Borgogna Designer: Angelo Sganzerla
7911	Mammut Costruzioni Designer: Angelo Sganzerla
7912	Mario Monti Editore Designer: Angelo Sganzerla
7913	New York City, Department of Parks and Recreation Designer: D. Bruce Zahor
7914	Why Weight, Jesse S. Miller, Ph. D. & Jacqueline A. Smith, Ph. D. Designer: D. Bruce Zahor
7915	Brachet's Jazz Restaurant Designer: D. Bruce Zahor
7916	Hypnosis Training Institute Designer: D. Bruce Zahor
7917	American Express Company, Learning Resource Center Designer: D. Bruce Zahor
7918	Grand Central Racquetball Club Designer: D. Bruce Zahor

 7919

 7923

 7920

 7924

 7921

 7925

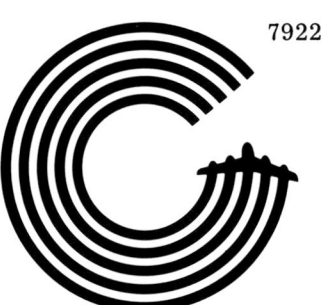 7922

 7926

7927

7928

7919	Progressive Grocer Company	
	Designer: D. Bruce Zahor	
7920	A.J. Wildman & Son, Inc.	
	Designer: D. Bruce Zahor	
7921	Leif Hope's Laundry Restaurant	
	Designer: D. Bruce Zahor	
7922	Command Travel Inc.	
	Designer: D. Bruce Zahor	
7923	A Choice in Therapy	
	Designer: D. Bruce Zahor	
7924	International Women's Writing Guild	
	Designer: D. Bruce Zahor	
7925	Tenth House Enterprises Inc.	
	Designer: D. Bruce Zahor	
7926	The Learning Store Ltd.	
	Designer: D. Bruce Zahor	
7927	Lincoln Financial Corporation	
	Designer: Ted Baptista	
7928	Rainbow Camera	
	Designer: Ted Baptista	
7929	Magnum Transportation	
	Designer: Ted Baptista	
7930	Dawn Marie Skin Care Center	
	Designer: Ted Baptista	

7929

7930

7931

7935

7932

7936

7933

7937

7934

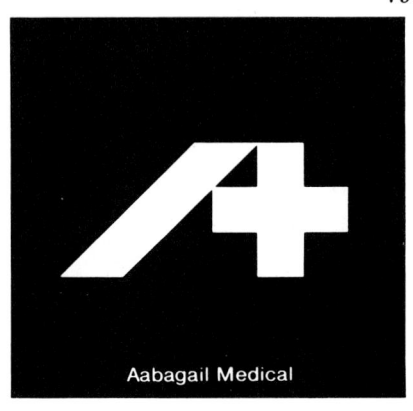
7938

7939

7940

7941

7942

7931	Vintage Cars	
	Designer: Ted Baptista	
7932	The Housing Coalition	
	Designer: Ted Baptista	
7933	Aiea Optical	
	Designer: Ted Baptista	
7934	Aloha State Realty	
	Designer: Ted Baptista	
7935	Surf Tours	
	Designer: Ted Baptista	
7936	Ackman-Yamamoto Opticians	
	Designer: Ted Baptista	
7937	Greenpeace	
	Designer: Ted Baptista	
7938	Aabagail Medical	
	Designer: Ted Baptista	
7939	Haena Shoes	
	Designer: Ted Baptista	
7940	Sheraton Maui Hotel	
	Designer: Ted Baptista	
7941	Consolidated Amusement	
	Designer: Ted Baptista	
7942	Solmar Development Company	
	Designer: Ted Baptista	

7943

7944

7945

7946

7947

7948

7949

7950

7951

7952

7953

7943	WBTV/Jefferson-Pilot Broadcasting Co. Designer: Joe Sonderman, Inc.
7944	Tomlinson Engineering Company Designer: Joe Sonderman, Inc.
7945	The Carlton (condominiums) Designer: Joe Sonderman, Inc.
7946	Roy White's Flowers Designer: Joe Sonderman, Inc.
7947	The Hilton Head Company Designer: Joe Sonderman, Inc.
7948	Charlotte Motor Speedway Designer: Joe Sonderman, Inc.
7949	Charlotte Speech & Hearing Center Designer: Joe Sonderman, Inc.
7950	Harwell Enterprises Designer: Joe Sonderman, Inc.
7951	Carolina Truck Centers, Inc. Designer: Joe Sonderman, Inc.
7952	One Eyed Tomcat, Inc. Designer: Joe Sonderman, Inc.
7953	The Charlotte Nature Museum Designer: Joe Sonderman, Inc.
7954	Pic 'n Pay Shoes, Inc. Designer: Joe Sonderman, Inc.

Pic 'n Pay 7954

7955

7956

7957

7958

7959

7960

7955	Leaf 'n Petal Designer: Joe Sonderman, Inc.
7956	Systems Associates, Inc. Designer: Joe Sonderman, Inc.
7957	Shipyard Plantation Designer: Joe Sonderman, Inc.
7958	Santa Cruz Community Credit Union Designer: Jane Burton Wagstaff
7959	Cuenca & Associates Designer: Jane Burton Wagstaff
7960	Olin and Wilson, Accountants Designer: Jane Burton Wagstaff
7961	The Camellia Syphony Orchestra Designer: Ron Fritz-Zavacki

7961

7962

EPICUREAN
COFFEE COMPANY

7966

7963

7967

7964

7968

7965

7969
beeffalo

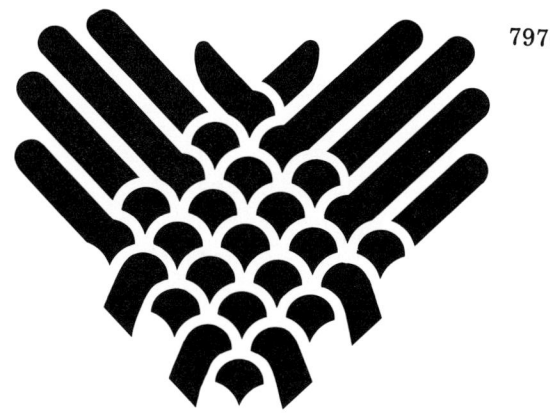

7962	Coffee Company	Designer: Ron Fritz-Zavacki
7963	David Butler Company	Designer: Ron Fritz-Zavacki
7964	Unger Construction Company	Designer: Ron Fritz-Zavacki
7965	Marketing by Design, Inc.	Designer: Ron Fritz-Zavacki
7966	Sacramento Film Festival	Designer: Ron Fritz-Zavacki
7967	Pickett-Rotholz and Murphy	Designer: Ron Fritz-Zavacki
7968	Lora Boylan, Interior Designer	Designer: Jane Burton Wagstaff
7969	Beeffalo (proposal)	Designer: Jane Burton Wagstaff
7970	Handweaver's Guild of America, Inc.	Designer: Carol Spain
7971	Shear Sensations	Designer: Joseph D. Waller
7972	Croix Media Communications	Designer: Kevin Heaton
7973	Clarken Enterprises	Designer: Don Sellars

7974

7978
Adega do Marquês.

7975

7979

7976

7980

7977

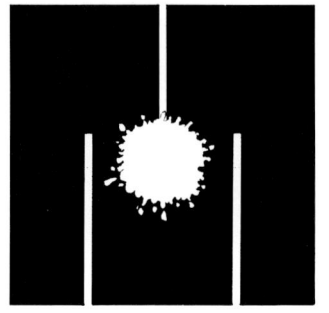
7981

7982

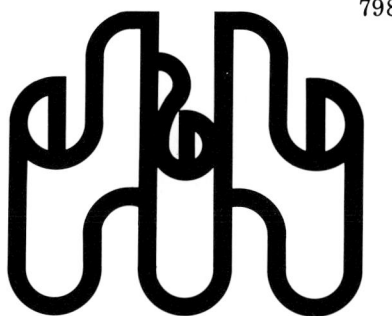

7983

7984

7985

7974	Radio Cidade	Designer: Oswald Miranda
7975	Senar	Designer: Oswald Miranda
7976	Posto Jumbo	Designer: Oswald Miranda
7977	Maracaju Veiculos	Designer: Oswald Miranda
7978	Adega do Marques	Designer: Oswald Miranda
7979	Clinica Anchieta	Designer: Oswald Miranda
7980	Casa dos Presentes	Designer: Oswald Miranda
7981	Miran-Marcas	Designer: Oswald Miranda
7982	Tipiti	Designer: Oswald Miranda
7983	Marli-bras	Designer: Oswald Miranda
7984	Vila Camoes	Designer: Oswald Miranda
7985	Bananas	Designer: Oswald Miranda

7986

7987

7988

7989

7986	Sketch	Designer: Oswald Miranda
7987	Ponto de Encontro	Designer: Oswald Miranda
7988	Sistema Urbano de Tracao Electrica	Designer: Oswald Miranda
7989	AECIC	Designer: Oswald Miranda
7990	Skeptic	Designer: Scott F. Reid
7991	McCullough & Sons Welldrilling	Designer: George Sierakowski
7992	Japan Ad-Art, Inc.	Designer: Masahiro Oishi
7993	Unitika Berkshire Co., Ltd.	Designer: Masahiro Oishi

7994

7998

7995

7999

7996

8000

7997

8001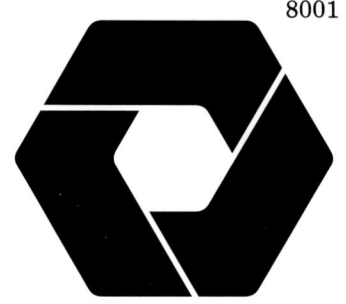

8002

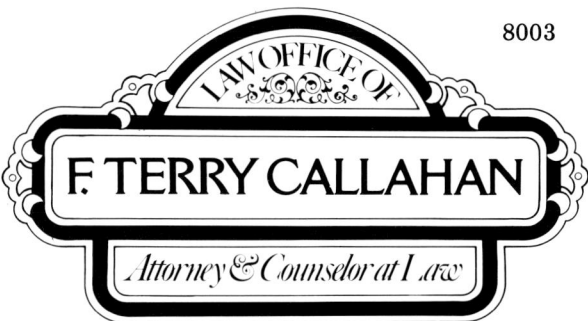

8003

8004

7994	Ad-Able Ltd. Designer: Masahiro Oishi
7995	Gallery Kashahara Designer: Masahiro Oishi
7996	Reitsport Ruhm Designer: Masahiro Oishi
7997	Hayashida Ltd. Designer: Masahiro Oishi
7998	Central Studio Designer: Masahiro Oishi
7999	Morishita Co., Ltd. Designer: Masahiro Oishi
8000	Salon de Gout Designer: Masahiro Oishi
8001	JFSA Designer: Masahiro Oishi
8002	Hidden Meadow Apartments Designer: Charlotte Potts
8003	F. Terry Callahan, Attorney and Counselor at Law Designer: Charlotte Potts
8004	Concord Properties Designer: Charlotte Potts

8005

8008
LOUISIANA
DATA
SERVICES, INC.

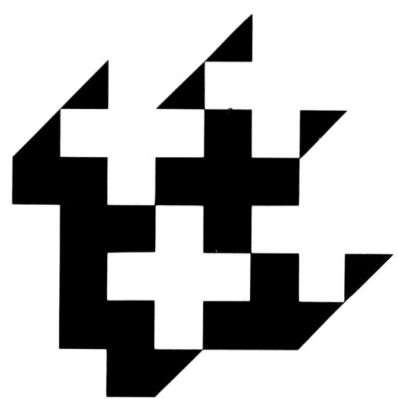

8006

8009
LANDMARK
ADVERTISING
INCORPORATED

8010

8007

8011

8012

8013

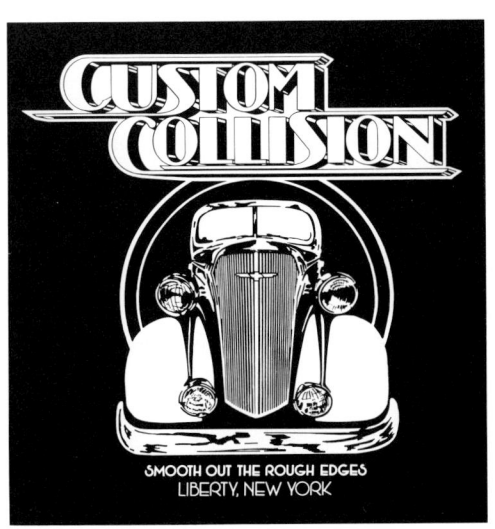

8014

8005	Charlotte Potts	Designer: Charlotte Potts
8006	Medical Properties	Designer: Charlotte Potts
8007	Care Inns	Designer: Charlotte Potts
8008	LDS, Inc.	Designer: Carlos M. Segura
8009	Landmark Advertising Incorporated	Designer: Carlos M. Segura
8010	Adanac	Designer: Jim Tweedy
8011	Brother Jacks	Designer: Thomas Ambrosino
8012	The Place	Designer: Thomas Ambrosino
8013	The Black Velvet Band	Designer: Thomas Ambrosino
8014	Custom Collison	Designer: Bev Thomas

8015

Genwall™

8019

8016

Spray Mist

8020

8017

Wallsource®

8021

8018

Vinyliner™

8022

8023

8024

8025

8026

8015   GTR Wallcovering Co.
Designer: Alan Wood Graphic Design, Inc.

8016   Neil Schiller
Designer: Alan Wood Graphic Design, Inc.

8017   GTR Wallcovering Co.
Designer: Alan Wood Graphic Design, Inc.

8018   Peter R. Paterson
Designer: Alan Wood Graphic Design, Inc.

8019   Neil Schiller
Designer: Alan Wood Graphic Design, Inc.

8020   Wood & Wong
Designer: Alan Wood Graphic Design, Inc.

8021   F.L. Russell Corp.
Designer: Alan Wood Graphic Design, Inc.

8022   Guma Footwear, Ltd.
Designer: Alan Wood Graphic Design, Inc.

8023   Barbara Buckley
Designer: Alan Wood Graphic Design, Inc.

8024   Bancomer (proposal)
Designer: Grupo Cuatro

8025   Rollerama
Designer: Grupo Cuatro

8026   Constructora Tabares
Designer: Grupo Cuatro

8027

8028

8030

8029

8031

8032

8033

8034

8035

8027	Ciudad Obregon Designer: Grupo Cuatro
8028	Grupo Baja Muk Designer: Grupo Cuatro
8029	Grupo Cuatro Designer: Grupo Cuatro
8030	Mid-America Dance Company, Wichita State University Designer: Dennis Ichiyama
8031	North Country Stove Works Designer: Len Eckel
8032	Sherlock Holmes (proposal) Designer: Dale McKinney
8033	Tiger Cub, Auburn University Designer: Dale McKinney
8034	Pocket Billiards, Red Scholefield Designer: Dale McKinney
8035	Sound Column Productions Designer: Randall Smith

8036

8037

8038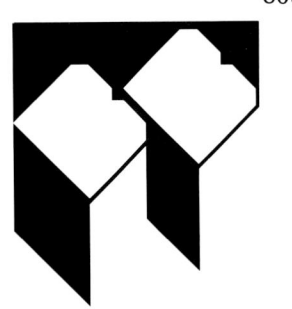

8039

8040

8041

8042

HUBERT SAWS

The GF Company

JDPRICE

8036	Back to Basics, Home food production & storage	Designer: Randall Smith
8037	Structural Systems	Designer: Randall Smith
8038	Bud Bailey Construction	Designer: Randall Smith
8039	Sell Your Own Home	Designer: Shelden Graphics
8040	John K. Landis Graphic Design	Designer: John K. Landis
8041	Van Nuys Travel Agencies	Designer: Sheldon Graphics
8042	Furniture Representive	Designer: Sheldon Graphics
8043	Saw Service	Designer: Sheldon Graphics
8044	Architectural Design Firm	Designer: Sheldon Graphics
8045	Construction Co.	Designer: Sheldon Graphics
8046	Auto Appraisers	Designer: Sheldon Graphics

M⊙

YOUR SIERRA NEVADA MUSEUM OF ART

8047

Reno International — 8048

antonia lowden — 8049

Nevada State Council on the Arts — 8050

8047	Sierra Nevada Museum of Art	Designer: Ron Taft
8048	Reno International Airport	Designer: Ron Taft
8049	Antonia Lowden Fiber Design	Designer: Ron Taft
8050	Nevada Council on the Arts	Designer: Ron Taft
8051	Coast Village Plaza	Designer: James F. Palam
8052	Garcia Architects	Designer: James F. Palam
8053	Westpac Interiors	Designer: James F. Palam
8054	Carisma	Designer: James F. Palam

8055

8059

8056

8060

8057

8058

8061

8062

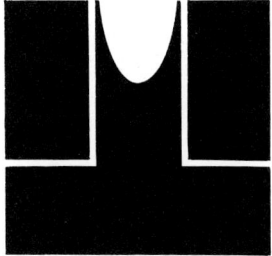

8063

8064

8065

8055	Bifano's	Designer: James F. Palam
8056	The Doneketesen	Designer: James F. Palam
8057	Santa Barbara Design/Build Incorporated	Designer: James F. Palam
8058	M-R Studios	Designer: Ed Bohon
8059	The Deciduous Press	Designer: Eugene Underwood
8060	Jackson County Family Life Council	Designer: John Pellicone
8061	Old Orchard Shopping Center	Designer: Richard D. Henderson
8062	Traffic Associates	Designer: Richard D. Henderson
8063	Alliance for the Mentally Ill	Designer: Richard D. Henderson
8064	Monogram or symbol for the name Joy	Designer: Richard D. Henderson
8065	Air Brake Specialists	Designer: Richard D. Henderson

8066

8067

8069

8068

8070

8071

8072

8073

8066	Sal's Pizzaroma Designer: David Bullock	
8067	David and Nora Bullock, Graphic Design/Illustration Designer: David Bullock	
8068	Chicory Hills Development Designer: David Bullock	
8069	Callowhill Citizens Assoc., Inc. Designer: David Bullock	
8070	Avondale Community Action Designer: Don Connelly & Associates	
8071	Giraf Grafix Designer: Don Connelly & Associates	
8072	Trans-America Corp. Designer: Don Connelly & Associates	
8073	Amtrak Designer: Lauren S. McDougal	

8074 PENNINGTON DESIGN

8078 HOUSING MANAGEMENT LTD.

8075 the community self-reliance center

8079 Gatty Communications inc.

8076 Thursday's coffeehouse

8077 One of the world's best theater companies is just around the corner.

8080 HOUSING fact sheets

8074	Pennington Design	Designer: Lauren S. McDougal
8075	The Community Self-Reliance Center	Designer: Lauren S. McDougal
8076	Cornell University	Designer: Lauren S. McDougal
8077	Arena Stage	Designer: Lauren S. McDougal
8078	Housing Management Ltd.	Designer: Lauren S. McDougal
8079	Gatty Communications, Inc.	Designer: Lauren S. McDougal
8080	New York State Cooperative Extension	Designer: Lauren S. McDougal
8081	National Association of Counties	Designer: Lauren S. McDougal
8082	The Wearhouse	Designer: Lauren S. McDougal
8083	Amtrak	Designer: Lauren S. McDougal
8084	Avanti	Designer: Lauren S. McDougal

8085

8086

8087

8088
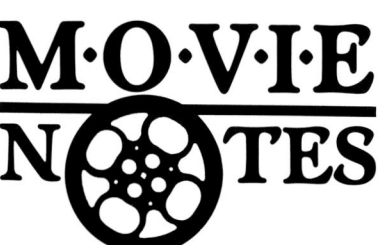

8089

8090

8091

8092

8093

8094

8085	Amtrak	
	Designer: Lauren S. McDougal	
8086	Living Quarters, Inc.	
	Designer: Lauren S. McDougal	
8087	G & G Specialties	
	Designer: Charles J. Wahlberg	
8088-8096	Arkansas Gazette	
	Designer: C. Spencer Morris	

 8095

 8097

 8096

 8098

 8099

8100

8101

8102

8103

8097	The Minnesota Automobile Dealers Association Designer: Susan M. Ahbe	
8098	The Sisk Company Inc. Designer: John R. Anglim	
8099	The Sisk Company Inc. Designer: John R. Anglim	
8100	Commons at Mendham Designer: Stephanie Grimaldi	
8101	The Acorn Lodge Designer: Stephanie Grimaldi	
8102	Snugglers' Hearth, Vermont Designer: Stephanie Grimaldi	
8103	Medical Economics Co. Designer: Stephanie Grimaldi	

8104

8108

8105

8109

8106

8110

8107

8111

8104	Quali-T Automotive	Designer: Stephanie Grimaldi
8105	Springdale	Designer: Stephanie Grimaldi
8106	L. Rosen Productions	Designer: Stephanie Grimaldi
8107	United Wire Hanger	Designer: Stephanie Grimaldi
8108	S. Grimaldi	Designer: Stephanie Grimaldi
8109	Laurel Hill	Designer: Stephanie Grimaldi
8110	R. Del Guercio, Inc.	Designer: Stephanie Grimaldi
8111	Preakness Gourmet Deli	Designer: Stephanie Grimaldi
8112	Franklin State Bank	Designer: Stephanie Grimaldi
8113	Clearwater Village	Designer: Stephanie Grimaldi
8114	Southern California Department of Water And Power	Designer: Larry Locke
8115	Bob Banner and Associates	Designer: Larry Locke

8116

8120

8117

8121
SCRF

8118
atoms

8122

8119

8123

8124

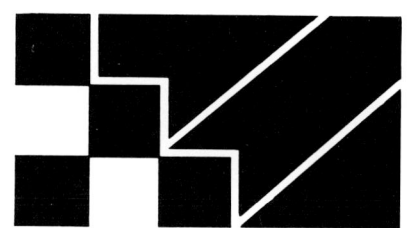

8125

8126

8127

8116	Imed Corporation	Designer: HumanGraphic
8117	Voyager	Designer: HumanGraphic
8118	Atoms	Designer: HumanGraphic
8119	Hungry Mouth	Designer: HumanGraphic
8120	Steppin' Out	Designer: HumanGraphic
8121	Scripps Clinic and Research Foundation	Designer: HumanGraphic
8122	Piktor's Metamorphosis, Inc.	Designer: HumanGraphic
8123	Dirt	Designer: HumanGraphic
8124	Quigley	Designer: HumanGraphic
8125	British Racing Motors	Designer: Theodore Alexander, Jr.
8126	A. I. Friedman	Designer: Theodore Alexander, Jr.
8127	The Watch Works	Designer: Theodore Alexander, Jr.

8128

8132

8129

8133

8130

8134

8131

8135

8128	Electrol, S.A.	
	Designer: Morfos Diseno, S.C.	
8129	Sahitur, Tabasco	
	Designer: Morfos Diseno, S.C.	
8130	Lopez Guerra Arquitectos, S. C.	
	Designer: Morfos Diseno, S.C.	
8131	Perforadora Mexico, S.A.	
	Designer: Morfos Diseno, S.C.	
8132	Software International, S.A.	
	Designer: Morfos Diseno, S.C.	
8133	Incubadora Cajeme, S.C.	
	Designer: Morfos Diseno, S.C.	
8134	Transportes Kinematos, S.A. de C.V.	
	Designer: Morfos Diseno, S.C.	
8135	Tilysa	
	Designer: Morfos Diseno, S.C.	
8136	Sahitur, Tabasco	
	Designer: Morfos Diseno, S.C.	
8137	Sahitur, Tabasco	
	Designer: Morfos Diseno, S.C.	
8138	Sahitur, Tabasco	
	Designer: Morfos Diseno, S.C.	

8139

8143

8140

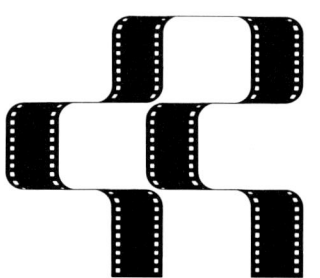

8141

8142

8144

8145

8146

8147

8148

8149

	8139	Administradora Tzocotumbac, S.A. Designer: Morfos Diseno, S.C.
	8140	Comision Latinoamericana de Administracion para el Desarrollo Designer: Ricardo Benaim
	8141	Cineautos Nacionales C.A. Designer: Ricardo Benaim
	8142	I Congreso Latinoamericano de Neurocirugia Designer: Ricardo Benaim
	8143	Corporacion de Turismo de Venezuela Designer: Ricardo Benaim
	8144	OTEARCA (Compania Constructora) Designer: Ricardo Benaim
	8145	Kissin' Her Pub Designer: Ricardo Benaim
	8146	Cardamation Designer: Trish Donahey
	8147	Communique Designer: Trish Donahey
	8148	Starfire Designer: Trish Donahey
	8149	Fieldstone Designer: Trish Donahey
	8150	Nurion Designer: Trish Donahey

8150

8151
American Graphics

8155

8152

8156

8157

8153

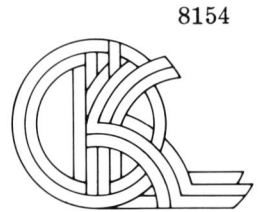
8154

8158

8159

8160

8161

8162

8151	American Graphics	Designer: Trish Donahey
8152	Three Bears, ice cream parlor	Designer: Trish Donahey
8153	Palmas del Mar	Designer: Trish Donahey
8154	Casual Kut	Designer: Trish Donahey
8155	Jo, artist	Designer: Trish Donahey
8156	CDQ Printing	Designer: Trish Donahey
8157	Trish, designer	Designer: Trish Donahey
8158	Pioneer Products	Designer: Trish Donahey
8159	No client listed	Designer: Trish Donahey
8160	Building firm	Designer: Trish Donahey
8161	F.L. Stephens	Designer: Trish Donahey
8162	Indian Fetish, Indian jewelry	Designer: Trish Donahey

8163

8167

graphic impressions.

8164

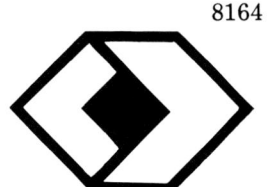

8168

casual kut

8165

8169

8166

8170

Philadelphia Area Newsletter
MSIA

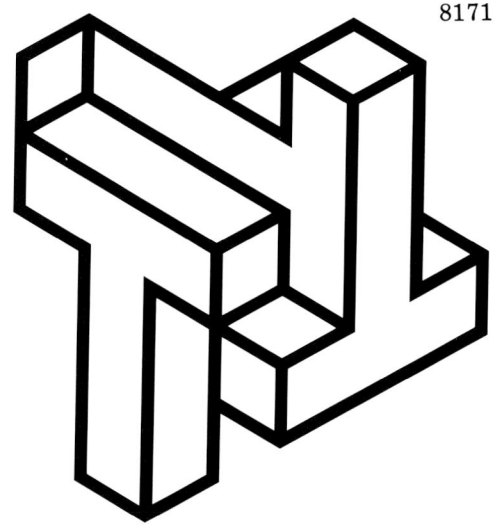

8171

8172

8163	Carder Company	Designer: Trish Donahey
8164	Carder Company	Designer: Trish Donahey
8165	Parke Institute	Designer: Trish Donahey
8166	The Type Factory	Designer: Trish Donahey
8167	Graphic Impressions	Designer: Trish Donahey
8168	Casual Kut	Designer: Trish Donahey
8169	Strike One	Designer: Trish Donahey
8170	Philadelphia Area Newsletter	Designer: Trish Donahey
8171	IDS Tax-Empt Bond Fund symbol	Designer: Gale William Ikola
8172	Minnesota Orchestral Association 75th symbol	Designer: Gale William Ikola

SKAGGS 8173

strome 8174

8175

8176

8177

8173	Designers Logotype Designer: Steven Skaggs
8174	Strome Inc. Designer: Steven Skaggs
8175	Symbol for children in America exhibit Designer: Steven Skaggs
8176	Georgia Hospital Association Designer: Steven Skaggs
8177	Capella choral group with Seed and Feed Theatre Designer: Steven Skaggs
8178	Gift shop at the High Museum of Art, Atlanta Designer: Steven Skaggs
8179	Nova Art Consultants Designer: Steven Skaggs

8178

8179

8180

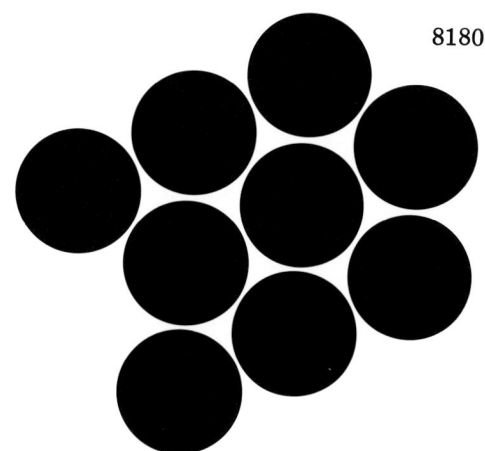

8183

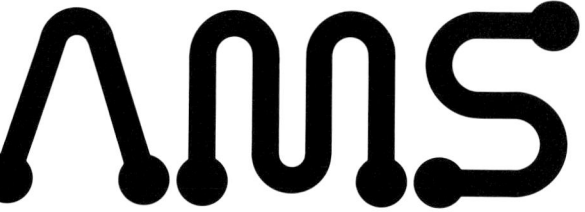

8184

THE WHOLE
SHOOTIN'
MATCH

8181

8185

8182

The Great
SouthEast
MUSIC HALL
EMPORIUM &
PERFORM-
ING ARTS
EXCHANGE
INC.

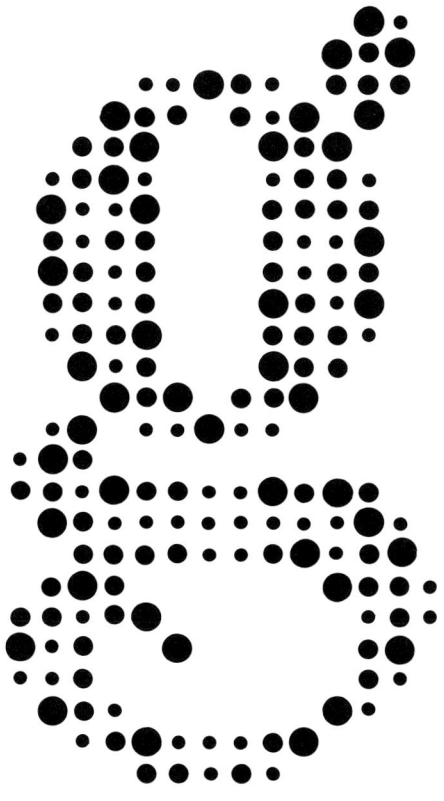

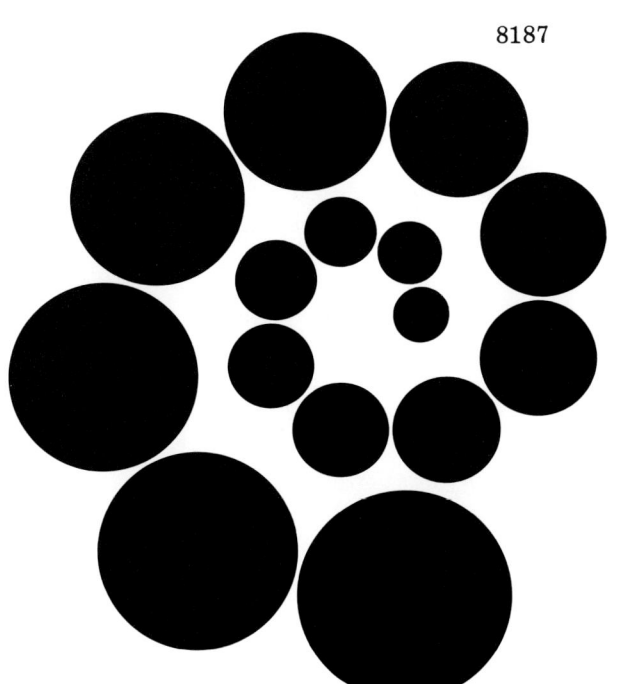

8180	Staten Island Children's Museum Designer: Steven Skaggs
8181	Carl Nelson, graphic designer Designer: Carl Nelson
8182	AMS, Inc. Designer: Carl Nelson
8183	SYCOM, Inc. Designer: Carl Nelson
8184	"The Whole Shootin' Match" Designer: Carl Nelson
8185	The Great South East Music Hall Emporium & Performing Arts Exchange, Inc. Designer: Robert P. Gersin Associates, Inc.
8186	Gucker & Goldstein Inc. Designer: Robert P. Gersin Associates, Inc.
8187	Pearlridge Mall Designer: Robert P. Gersin Associates, Inc.

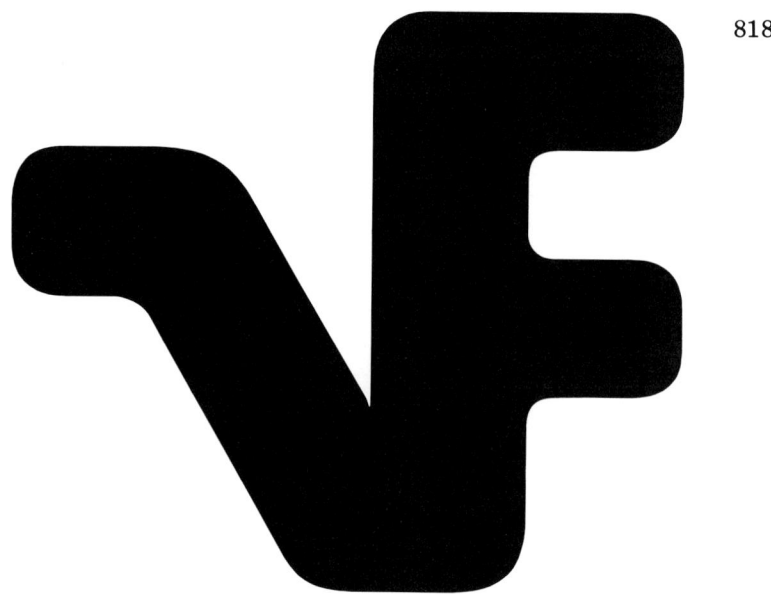

8188

8189

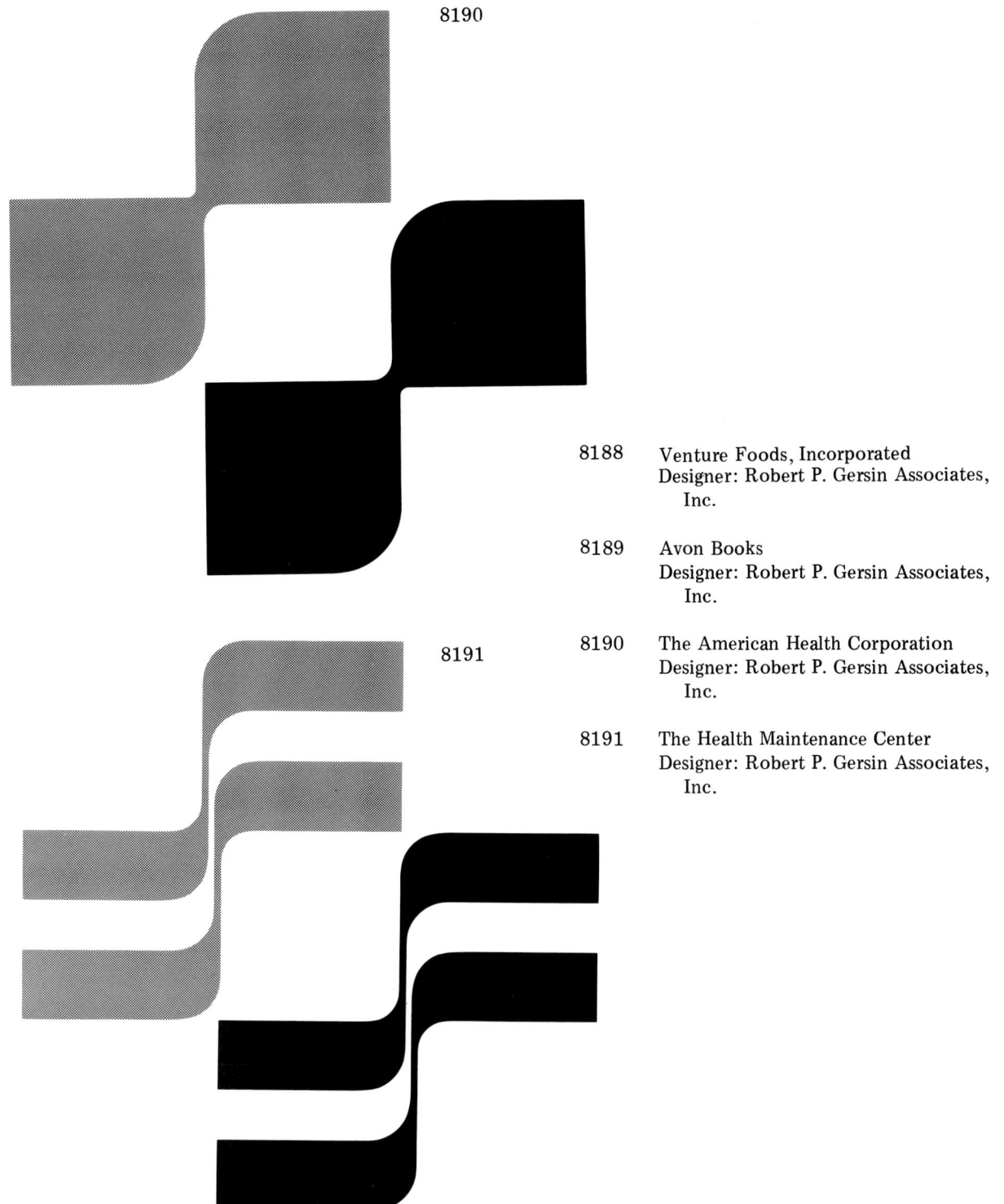

8188 Venture Foods, Incorporated
      Designer: Robert P. Gersin Associates, Inc.

8189 Avon Books
      Designer: Robert P. Gersin Associates, Inc.

8190 The American Health Corporation
      Designer: Robert P. Gersin Associates, Inc.

8191 The Health Maintenance Center
      Designer: Robert P. Gersin Associates, Inc.

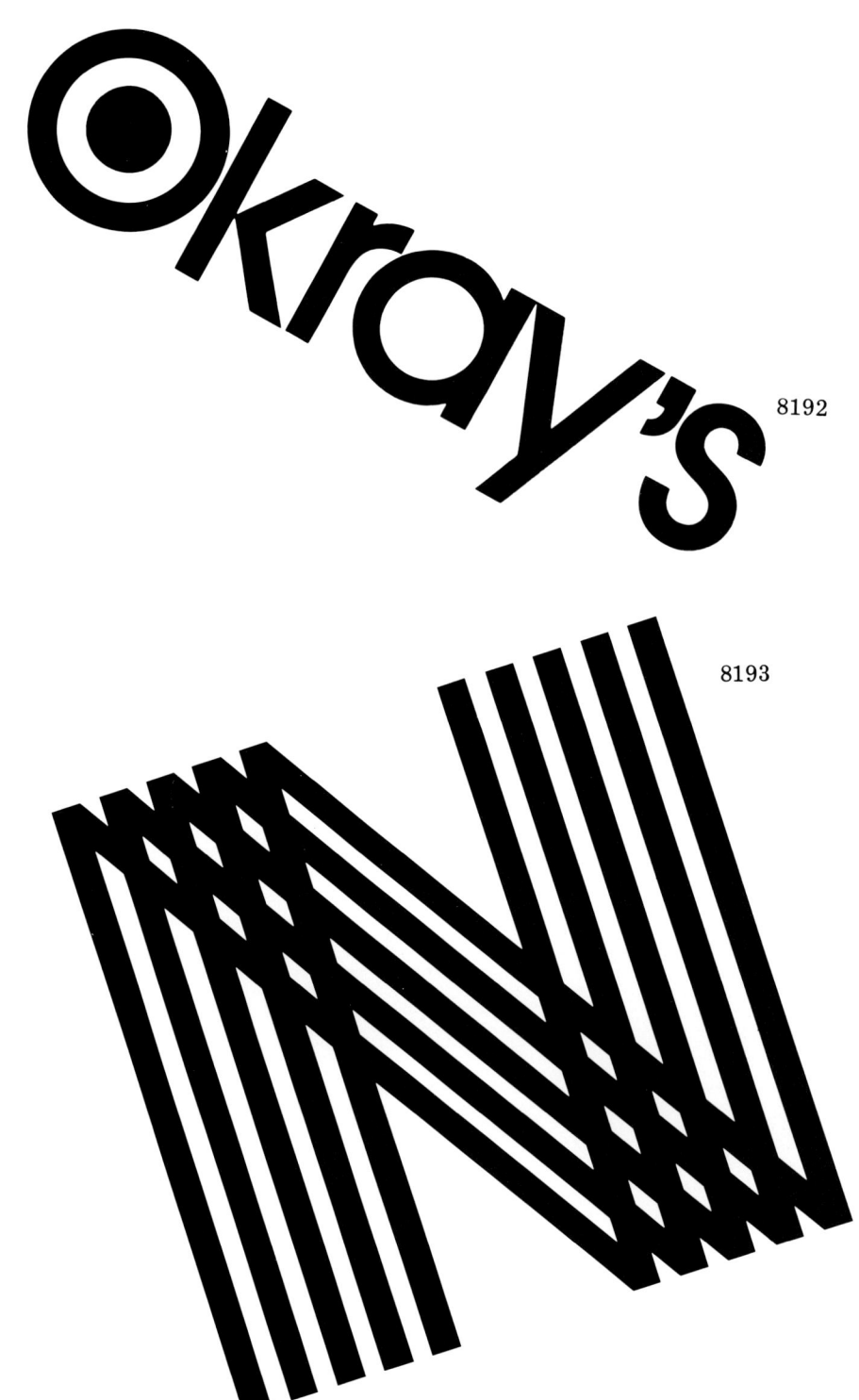

8192

8193

8192 Okray's
Designer: Robert P. Gersin Associates, Inc.

8193 National Shirt Shops
Designer: Robert P. Gersin Associates, Inc.

8194 Isseks Brothers, Inc.
Designer: Robert P. Gersin Associates, Inc.

8195 The Technition Group
Designer: Robert P. Gersin Associates, Inc.

8196

8197

8198

8199

8200

8196   Connecticut Off-Track Betting
Designer: Robert P. Gersin Associates, Inc.

8197   BVD Company, Union Underwear Co.
Designer: Robert P. Gersin Associates, Inc.

8198   Broward Mall
Designer: Robert P. Gersin Associates, Inc.

8199   Woodfield Mall
Designer: Robert P. Gersin Associates, Inc.

8200   Eastridge Mall
Designer: Robert P. Gersin Associates, Inc.

"No nonsense® panty hose"

8201

WOLF

8202

8203

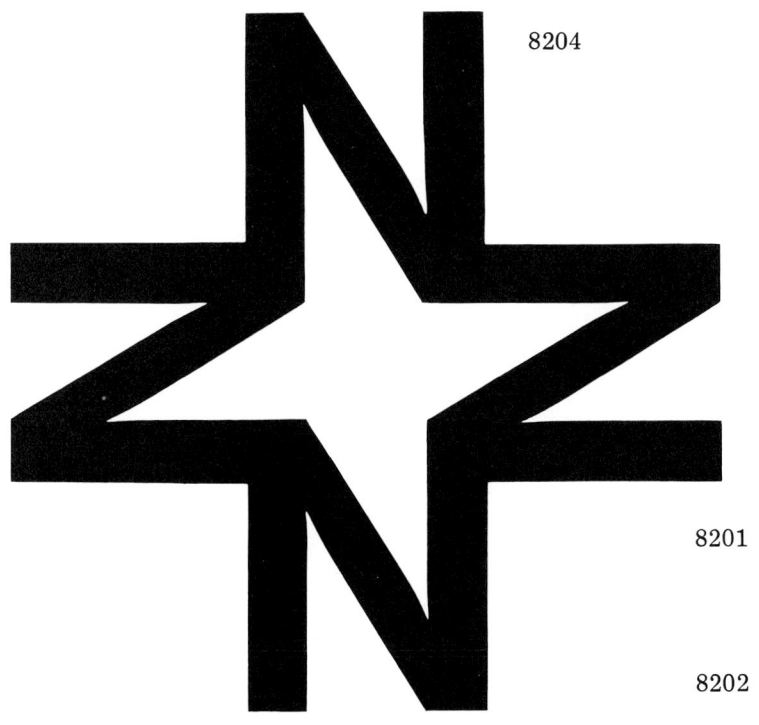

8204

8205

8201	Kayser-Roth Hosiery Co., Inc.- No Nonsense Designer: Robert P. Gersin Associates, Inc.
8202	E.J. Wolf Designer: Robert P. Gersin Associates, Inc.
8203	Saratoga Performing Arts Center, Inc. Designer: Robert P. Gersin Associates, Inc.
8204	Northridge Mall Designer: Robert P. Gersin Associates, Inc.
8205	AT&T Designer: Robert P. Gersin Associates, Inc.

8206

8207

8209

8208

8210

8206	Flexnit Co., Inc.	
	Designer: Robert P. Gersin Associates, Inc.	
8207	Linda Prusse-Creative Services	
	Designer: Gordon Gutke	
8208	Ad-Centives West, Inc.	
	Designer: Gordon Gutke	
8209	Great Basin Realty	
	Designer: Gordon Gutke	
8210	Frisco Electronics	
	Designer: Gordon Gutke	
8211	Stingers- Salt Lake City Pro Volleyball	
	Designer: Gordon Gutke	
8212	Toyota Dealers Assn.	
	Designer: Gordon Gutke	
8213	Toyota Dealers Assn.	
	Designer: Gordon Gutke	
8214	Kappa Corp.	
	Designer: Gordon Gutke	

8215

8219

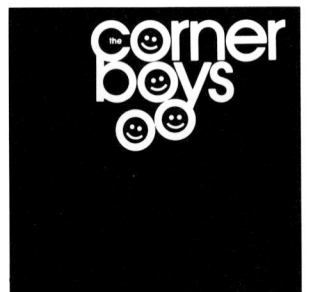
8216

8220

8221

8217

8218 8222

8223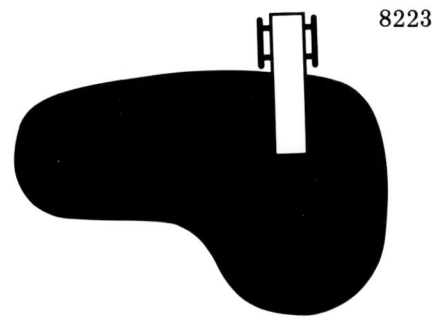

8224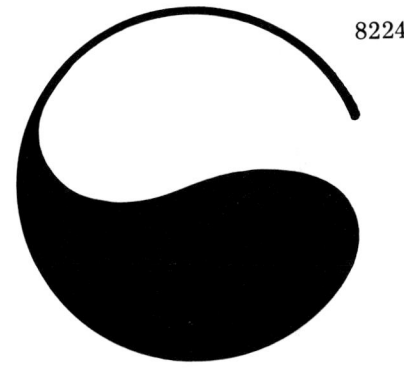

8225

8226

8215	Rainbow Rentals	Designer: Gordon Gutke
8216	The Corner Boys	Designer: Gordon Gutke
8217	Belmont Springs	Designer: Gordon Gutke
8218	Garden Gate Restaurant	Designer: Gordon Gutke
8219	LDS Church	Designer: Gordon Gutke
8220	Seminars on success	Designer: Gordon Gutke
8221	American Red Cross (Golden Spike Division)	Designer: Gordon Gutke
8222	Ireco Chemicals	Designer: Gordon Gutke
8223	Certified Pool Corp.	Designer: Gordon Gutke
8224	CS Enterprises (proposal)	Designer: Gordon Gutke
8225	HP Enterprises	Designer: Gordon Gutke
8226	Petersen-Gasser & Associates	Designer: Gordon Gutke

8227

8231

8228

8232

8229

8233

8230

8234

8227	Glacier Raft Company	Designer: Gordon Gutke
8228	Lorraine Press (proposal)	Designer: Gordon Gutke
8229	Condominium Concepts	Designer: Gordon Gutke
8230	Crown Toyota	Designer: Gordon Gutke
8231	Zeigler Engineering Sales, Inc.	Designer: Gordon Gutke
8232	Sun International Inc.	Designer: Gordon Gutke
8233	Boar's Head Restaurant, Continental Restaurant System, Inc.	Designer: Tom Lewis
8234	Ocean Garden Products, Inc.	Designer: Sandy Holman & Tom Lewis
8235	Carter Seeds	Designer: Tom Lewis
8236	Mission Chemical	Designer: Tom Lewis
8237	Bergquist Construction & Designs	Designer: John M. Alexander
8238	John E. King Tax Consultant	Designer: John M. Alexander

8239

8243

8240

8244

8241

8245

8242

8246
BirnamWoodGolfClub

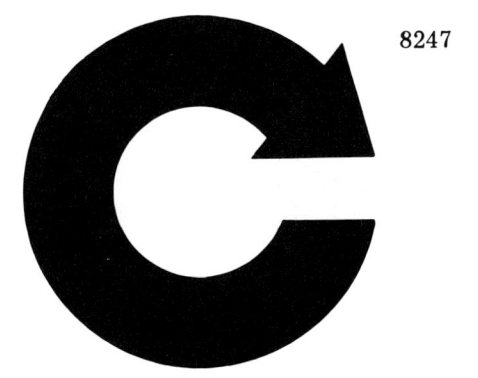

8247

8248

8239	Outsiders for Leather Ltd. Designer: John M. Alexander
8240	Casey Jones Bar Designer: John M. Alexander
8241	Beer Blanket for Leather Ltd. Designer: John M. Alexander
8242	Award 78 for the Greater Santa Barbara Advertising Federation Designer: John M. Alexander
8243	Terra Craft for Terra Craft Corporation Designer: John M. Alexander
8244	Sun-Pacific Properties Designer: John M. Alexander
8245	Safety Floaters for Leather Ltd. Designer: John M. Alexander
8246	Birnam Wood Golf Club Designer: John M. Alexander
8247	Circulation Tools, Inc. Designer: William Baronet
8248	Filteration Systems, Inc. Designer: William Baronet
8249	Pat Olson Designer: William Baronet
8250	Rotary Specialties, Inc. Designer: William Baronet

8249

8250

 8251

 8255

 8252

 8256

 8253

 8257

 8254

 8258

8259

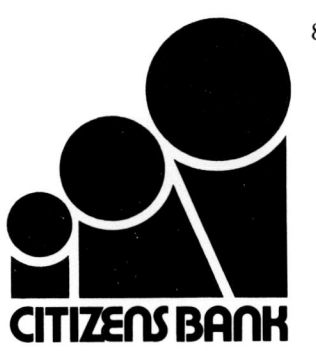

8260

8261

8262

8251	Oil Field	Designer: William Baronet
8252	Lamarco Insurance	Designer: William Baronet
8253	Globe Tel Aviv — Travel Service Ltd.	Designer: Ilan Peeri
8254	Merrill Lynch Property Development	Designer: Thomas J. Graham
8255	Brown & Williamson International Tobacco	Designer: Thomas J. Graham
8256	Elizabethtown City Schools	Designer: Thomas J. Graham
8257	Charles Restaurant	Designer: Thomas J. Graham
8258	B & S Glassworks	Designer: Thomas J. Graham
8259	Elizabethtown, Ky.	Designer: Thomas J. Graham
8260	Brown and Williamson International	Designer: Thomas J. Graham
8261	Tell Tale Sales	Designer: Thomas J. Graham
8262	Aurora	Designer: Arthur Eckstein

8263

trendleader

8264

LET BYGONES BE!

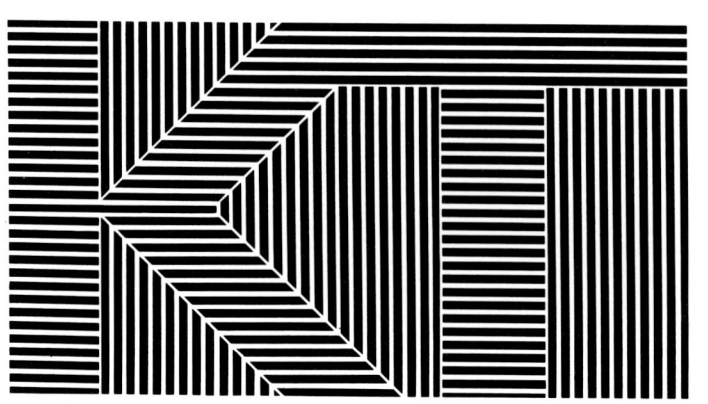

8265

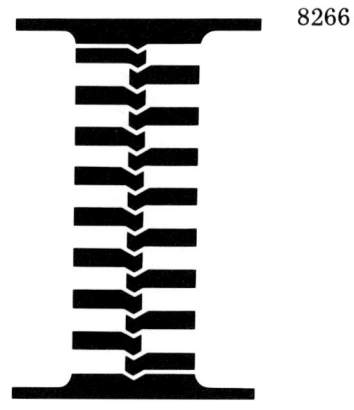

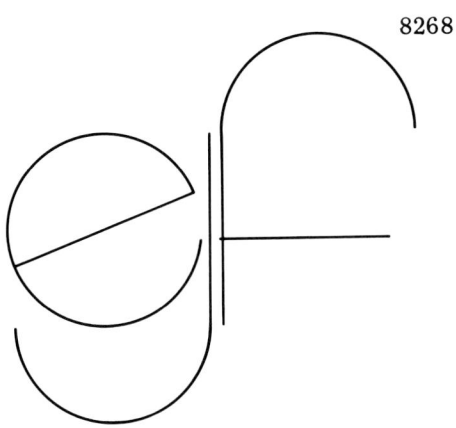

8263	The Lamport Co. Designer: Arthur Eckstein
8264	Let Bygones Be! - Antiques Designer: Arthur Eckstein
8265	Kent Typographic Service Designer: Ulla Rune/ Arthur Eckstein
8266	Ideal Fastener Corp. Designer: Arthur Eckstein
8267	Cheapskates Designer: Ellen J. Forstenzer
8268	EJF Graphic Design Designer: Ellen J. Forstenzer

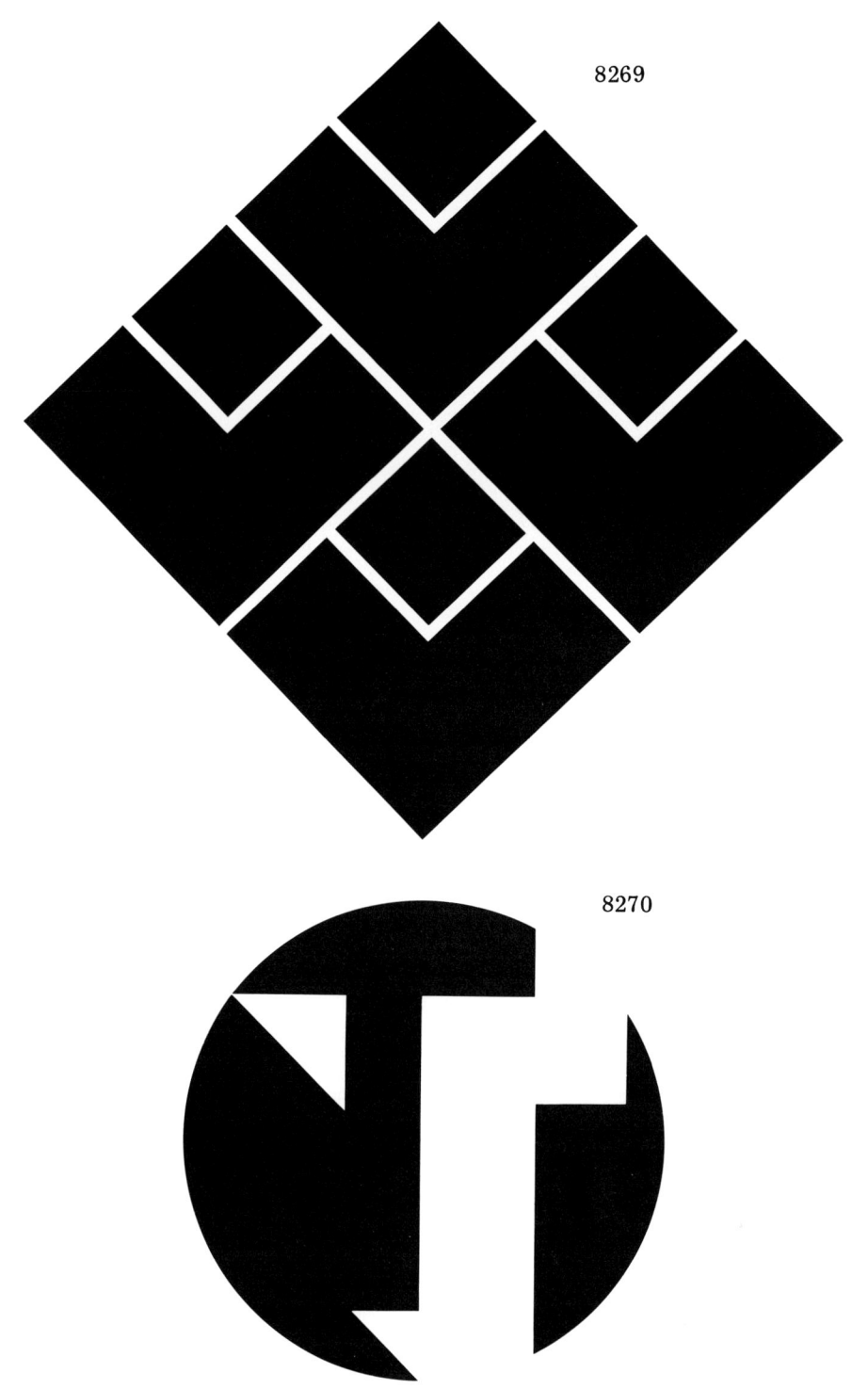

8269

8270

8271

VAX11 780

8272

8269	American Mining Congress Designer: Anthony Russell
8270	Teradyne Designer: David A. Lizotte
8271	Digital Equipment Corporation Designer: David A. Lizotte
8272- 8274	Avedis Zildjian Cymbal Company Designer: David A. Lizotte

8273

8274

8275

8276

8277

8278

8279

8275	Village Square Condominiums Designer: Clint Cline
8276	Master Broker Associates Designer: Clint Cline
8277	J & W Aircraft Maintenance Designer: Clint Cline
8278	Pinellas Apartment Association Designer: Clint Cline
8279	Associates in Physical Therapy Designer: Clint Cline
8280	Central Florida Multi Housing Association Designer: Clint Cline

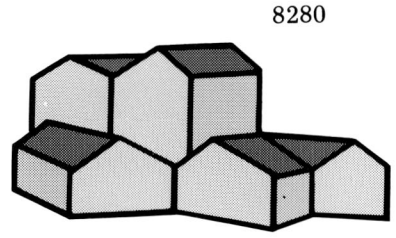
8280

8281

Habana Park

8285

8282

8286

8283
SUNWARD

8287

8284

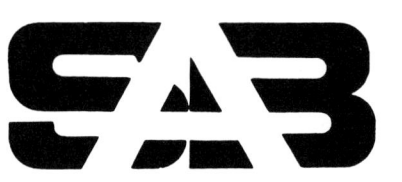
8288

8281	Habana Park Condominiums Designer: Clint Cline
8282	Littlefield Publishing Company, Inc. Designer: Clint Cline
8283	Sunward Investments, Inc. Designer: Chuck Allen
8284	Earth Resources Company Designer: Chuck Allen
8285	J.W. Sayles & Associates Designer: Chuck Allen
8286	Pencil Point Graphic Advertising Designer: Chuck Allen
8287	The Coffee House, East Texas State Univ. Designer: Chuck Allen
8288	Student Activity Board, East Texas State Univ. Designer: Chuck Allen
8289	Lake Park Gardens Designer: Chuck Allen
8290	Unpublished (Waterbeds) Designer: Chuck Allen
8291	Paddy Wack Apparel Designer: Chuck Allen
8292	Six Flags Over Texas Designer: Chuck Allen

8293

8297

8294

8298

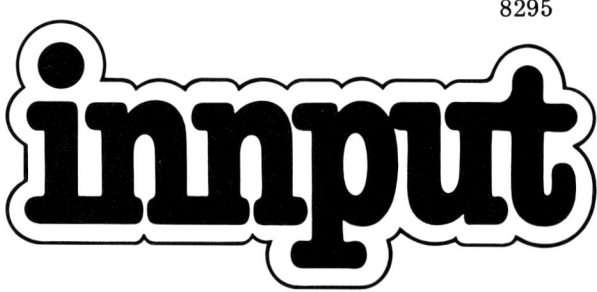
8295

8299

8296

8293	Meisel Photochrome Corp.	Designer: Chuck Allen
8294	Hallmark Institute	Designer: Chuck Allen
8295	La Quinta Motor Inns, Inc.	Designer: Chuck Allen
8296	Temple Emanual	Designer: Chuck Allen
8297	Bandit Enterprizes	Designer: Chuck Allen
8298	Technical & Marketing Services Corp.	Designer: Chuck Allen
8299	Six Flags Over Texas	Designer: Chuck Allen
8300	Tracsa	Designer: Jorge Canales, Javier de Leon
8301	Jorge Canales & Associates	Designer: Jorge Canales
8302	Comsemar, S.A.	Designer: Jorge Canales
8303	Alianza	Designer: Jorge Canales

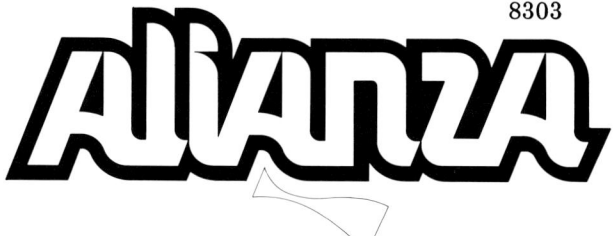

8304

8308

8305

8309

8306

8310

8307

8311

8312

8313

8314

8304	Banpesca	Designer: Jorge Canales
8305	Tenis Del Valle, S.A.	Designer: Jorge Canales
8306	Unica, S.A.	Designer: Jorge Canales
8307	Santiago Textil, S.A.	Designer: Jorge Canales
8308	Realist, Inc.	Designer: Timothy E. Urban
8309	AMF Harley-Davidson	Designer: Timothy E. Urban
8310	DeAvedon & Co.	Designer: Timothy E. Urban
8311	Fox River Paper Company	Designer: Timothy E. Urban
8312	Searle White Knight Textiles	Designer: Timothy E. Urban
8313	AMF Harley-Davidson	Designer: Timothy E. Urban
8314	California Association of Realtors	Designer: Gerry Rosentswieg

SAN PEDRO PENINSULA HOSPITAL 8315

8316
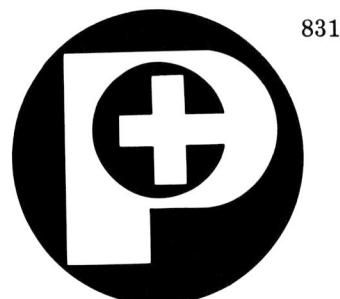

8317

8318

8319
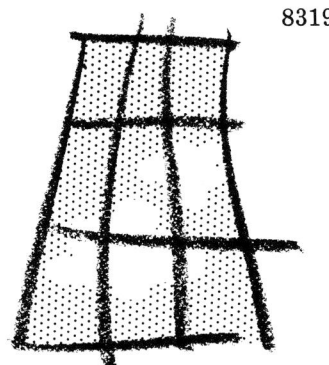

8320

8321

8322

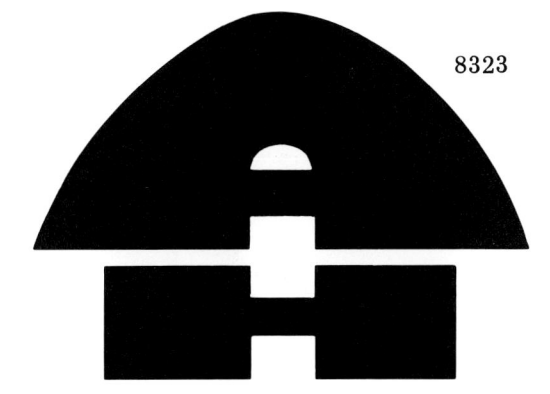

8323

8324

8315	San Pedro Peninsula Hospital Designer: Gerry Rosentswieg	
8316	Memorial Hospital of Panorama City Designer: Gerry Rosentswieg	
8317	Granada Hills Community Hospital- Children's Services Designer: Gerry Rosentswieg	
8318	Thalians Community Mental Health Center at Cedars-Sinai Medical Center Designer: Gerry Rosentswieg	
8319	Skylight Productions Designer: Gerry Rosentswieg	
8320	"The Sound of Children" Designer: Julie Ann Cairns	
8321	Emmanuel Carambola Grove Designer: Steve Allen	
8322	Ocean Flesh Designer: Steve Allen	
8323	Arlene Hawkins Cosmetics Designer: Humprey Sutherland	
8324	Arrow Maintenance Corp. Designer: Courtland Thomas White	
8325	Selective Marketing Service Group Designer: Courtland Thomas White	

8325

8326

8330

8327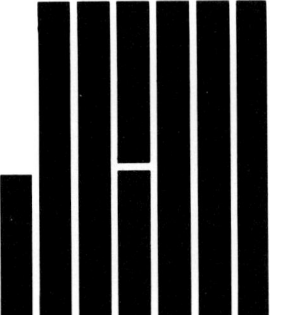

8331

8328

8332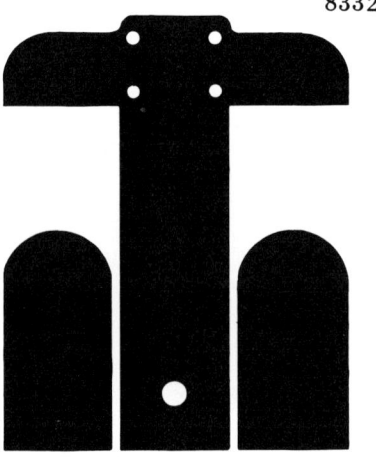

8329

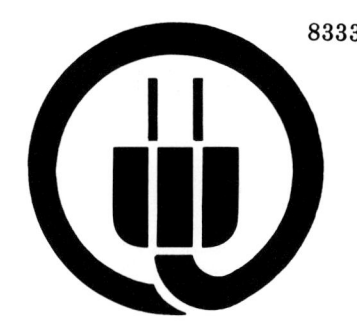

8333

8334

8326	Topper Toys Corp.	
	Designer: Courtland Thomas White	
8327	J.L. Marrow Lithographers	
	Designer: Courtland Thomas White	
8328	Target Promotions Inc.	
	Designer: Courtland Thomas White	
8329	United Neighborhood Houses of N.Y.	
	Designer: Courtland Thomas White	
8330	Thorton Hubburd School of Mixology	
	Designer: Courtland Thomas White	
8331	Milwaukee Metropolitan Sewage District	
	Designer: Ken Larsen	
8332	Terri Mesiti Graphic Design	
	Designer: Terri Mesiti	
8833	Wel-Don Appliance Service	
	Designer: Terri Mesiti	
8334-8340	Metropolitan Life Insurance Company	
	Designer: Stan Volinsky	

8335

8336

8340

8337

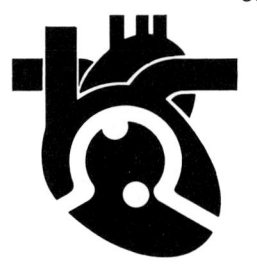
8341

8338

8342

8339

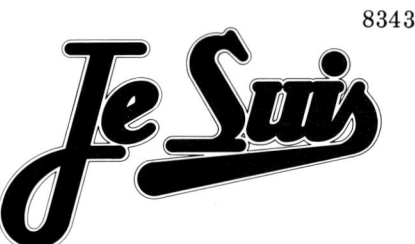
8343

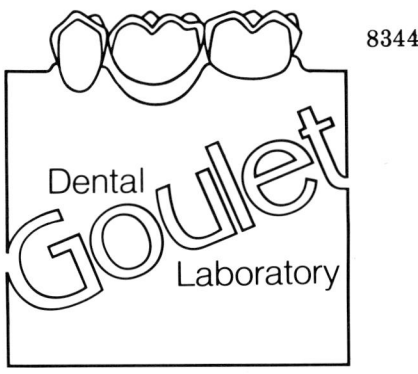

8341	Perfusion Service, Inc. Designer: William A. Latocki
8342	R.H. Swenarton Associates Designer: William A. Latocki
8343	JeSuis Unisex Salon Designer: William A. Latocki
8344	Goulet Dental Laboratory Designer: William A. Latocki
8345	Professional Theatre Program Designer: William A. Latocki
8346	Dapco Industries Designer: William A. Latocki
8347	Moldes Industriales Designer: Rion & Ezquerro y Asociados, S.C.

8348

Hospital Santelena

8352

M. Domit

8349

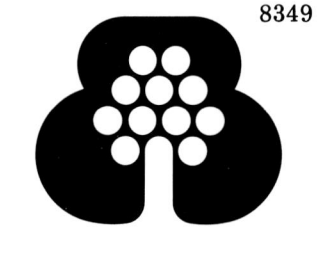

Plaza Bosques

8353

Domit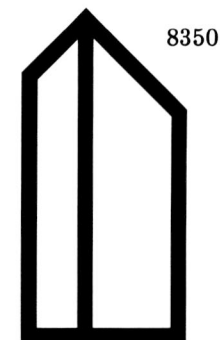

8350

Parque Reforma

8354

ACCIONES Y VALORES
DE MEXICO SA DE CV

8355

8351

InverMexico SA
CASA DE BOLSA

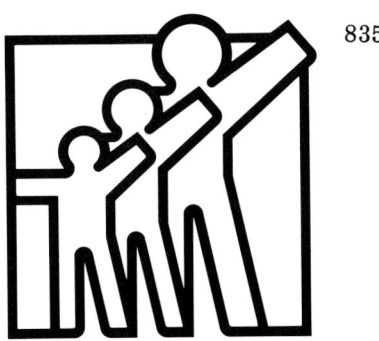

8356

8357

8358

8359

8348	Hospital Santelena	Designer: Rion & Ezquerro y Asociados, S.C.
8349	Plaza Bosques	Designer: Rion & Ezquerro y Asociados, S.C.
8350	Parque Reforma	Designer: Rion & Ezquerro y Asociados, S.C.
8351	InverMexico	Designer: Rion & Ezquerro y Asociados, S.C.
8352	M. Domit	Designer: Rion & Ezquerro y Asociados, S.C.
8353	Grupo Domit	Designer: Rion & Ezquerro y Asociados, S.C.
8354	Acciones y Valores de Mexico	Designer: Rion & Ezquerro y Asociados, S.C.
8355	Ultramag	Designer: Rion & Ezquerro y Asociados, S.C.
8356	Centro de Desarrollo de Personal	Designer: Rion & Ezquerro y Asociados, S.C.
8357	Helados Balam	Designer: Rion & Ezquerro y Asociados, S.C.
8358	Costa Coffee	Designer: Rion & Ezquerro y Asociados, S.C.
8359	The Little Apple Corporation	Designer: Douglas Korves

8360

WILD STRAWBERRIES

8361

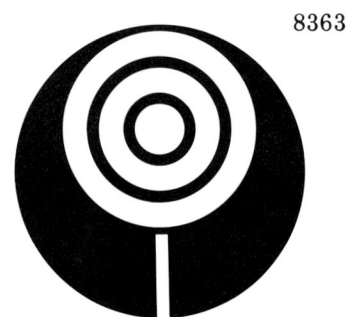

8363

Decorative

Candy

8362

8364

Crystal

Mens Shop

8365

Bath&Boudoir

8366

Ladies Apparel

8367

Casual Dining

8360	Wild Strawberries Designer: Anthony Aueles
8361- 8376	Halls Department Store Designer: Anthony Aueles

8368

Bridal

8371

Silver

8369

Host&Hostess

8372

EastRoom

8370

Information

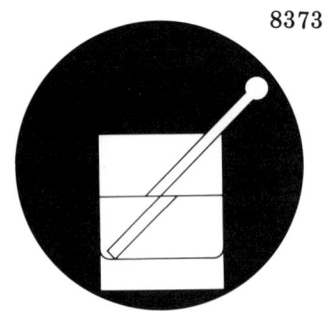
8373

BarAccessories

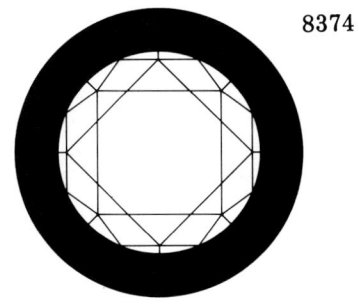

8374

FineJewelry

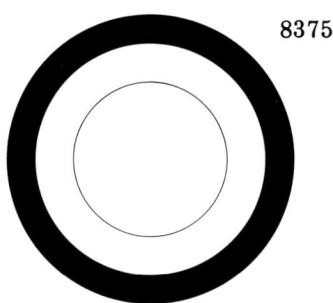

8375

8361-
8376 Halls Department Store
      Designer: Anthony Aueles

China

8376

Stationery

8377

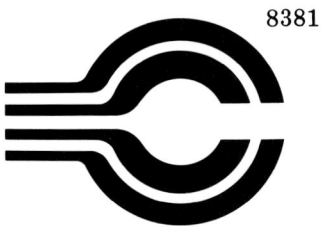

8381

8378

8382

8379

8383

8380

8384

8385

8386

8387

8388

8377	Cardinal Federal Savings & Loan Designer: Denise Spaulding
8378	Plaza Properties Designer: Denise Spaulding
8379	City Center Designer: Dave Carter
8380	American Federal Savings & Loan Designer: Denise Spaulding
8381	John W. Clark Oil Designer: Denise Spaulding
8382	Clark Gas Designer: Denise Spaulding
8383	Broward Federal Savings & Loan Designer: Denise Spaulding
8384	Robinson Excavating Designer: Denise Spaulding
8385	12 Week Diet Club Designer: Dave Carter
8386	Kach All Designer: Denise Spaulding
8387	WAMX Designer: Dave Carter
8388	Parts Depot Designer: Dave Carter

 8389

 8393

 8390

 8394

 8391

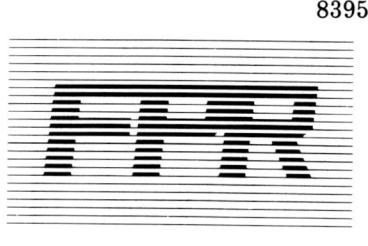 8395

 8392

 8396

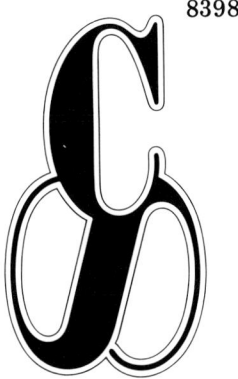

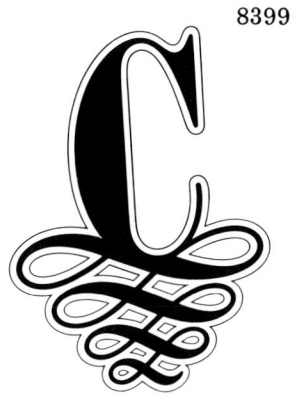

8389	Dorchester Corporation Designer: Denise Spaulding
8390	Kentucky Farmers Bank Designer: Denise Spaulding
8391	Tri-Medical Designer: Denise Spaulding
8392	David Osborne Designer: Denise Spaulding
8393	Home National Bank Designer: Denise Spaulding
8394	Boyd Service, Inc. Designer: Denise Spaulding
8395	FPR, Inc. Designer: Denise Spaulding
8396	American Back School Designer: Denise Spaulding
8397	Ashland Beverage Center Designer: Denise Spaulding
8398	Corematica-Computing Division Designer: Roberto Dosil & Mario Erkenazi Dosil & Erkenazi
8399	Corematica-Consulting in Administration Division Designer: Roberto Dosil & Mario Eskenazi Dosil & Erkenazi

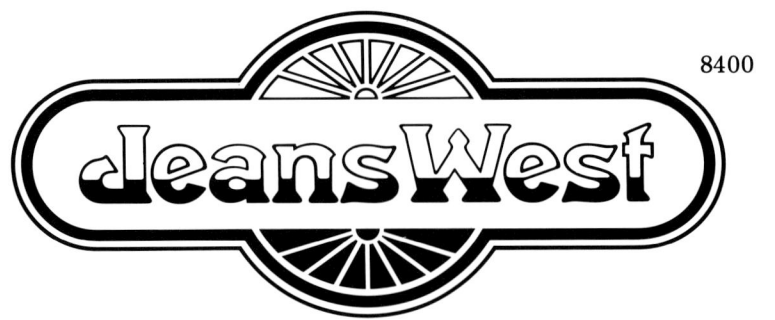

8400

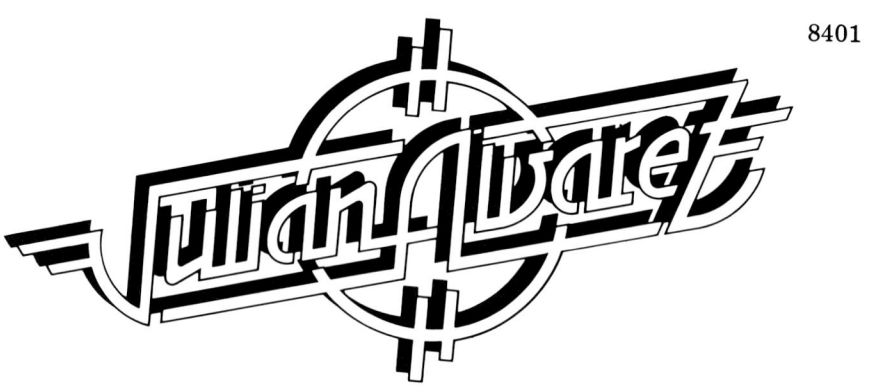

8401

8402

8403

8404

8405

8406

8400   JeansWest
Designer: Roberto Dosil
   Kent Allan Ltd.

8401   Julian Alvarez, illustrator
Designer: Roberto Dosil & Mario Eskenazi
   Dosil & Eskenazi

8402   Mario Eskenazi, graphic designer
Designer: Roberto Dosil & Mario Eskenazi
   Dosil & Eskenazi

8403   Eze Brew Coffee Service
Designer: Roberto Dosil
   Kent Allan Ltd.

8404   VIDEA-Victoria International Development Educational Association
Designer: Roberto Dosil
   Kent Allan Ltd.

8405   Roberto Dosil
Designer: Roberto Dosil & Mario Eskenazi
   Dosil & Eskenazi

8406   New World Learning System-Educational Kits
Designer: Roberto Dosil
   Kent Allan Ltd.

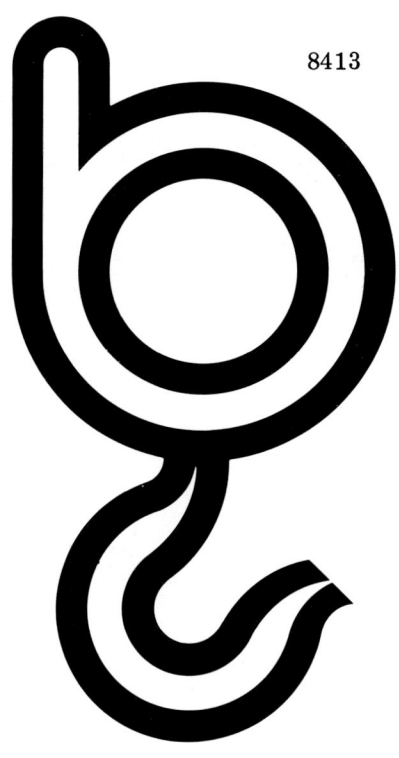

8413

8414

8407	University of British Columbia—International Intervisitation Program Designer: Roberto Dosil Kent Allan Ltd.
8408	Free Bus-Victoria City Hall Designer: Roberto Dosil Kent Allan Ltd.
8409	Foulger-Okland Company Designer: Jack Okland, Jr.
8410	Downtown Business Services, Inc. Designer: Jack Okland, Jr.
8411	Thomas Snowdon Associates, Inc. Designer: Jack Okland, Jr.
8412	Vivian S. Haas/illustrator Designer: Jack Okland, Jr.
8413	Butler Construction Co. Designer: Jack Okland, Jr.
8414	Brennan Construction Co., Inc. Designer: Jack Okland, Jr.

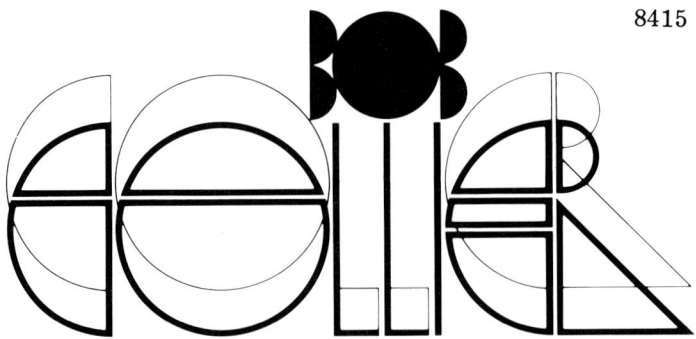

8415

8416

8417

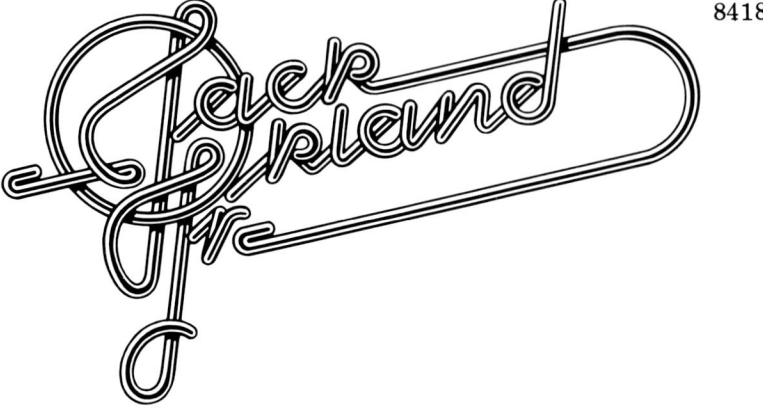

8418

8419

8420

8415	Bob Collier Enterprises Designer: Jack Okland, Jr.	
8416	The New York Pasta Co. Designer: Jack Okland, Jr.	
8417	The Aquarius Designer: Jack Okland, Jr.	
8418	Jack Okland, Jr./designer Designer: Jack Okland, Jr.	
8419	Pariscope Design Designer: Issac Paris Jr.	
8420	New Approach Method Designer: Issac Paris Jr.	

8421

mike+ike

8422

TerraCotta

Handmade Mexican Tiles, American Crafts, Gifts, Objects

8423

8424

8425

8421	Pariscope Design Designer: Issac Paris Jr.	
8422	Terra Cotta Designer: Issac Paris Jr.	
8423	Romance for Two Designer: Issac Paris Jr.	
8424	Prografic Designer: Fernando Medina	
8425	Sofico Vacaciones Designer: Fernando Medina	

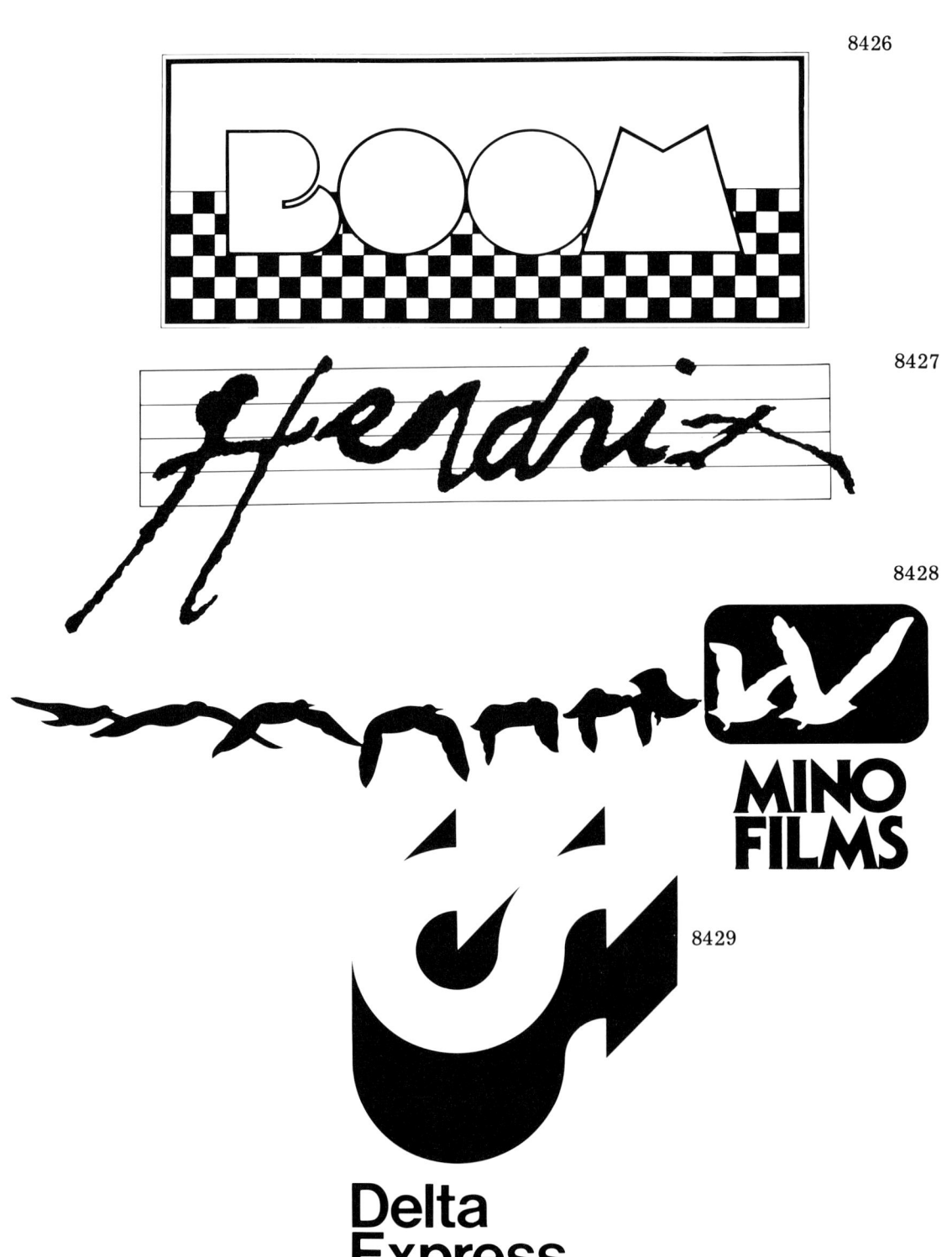

8430

The English Montessori School

8431

Banco Latino

8426	Boom Restaurant	Designer: Fernando Medina
8427	Musidora Films	Designer: Fernando Medina
8428	Mino Films	Designer: Fernando Medina
8429	Delta Express	Designer: Fernando Medina
8430	The English Montessori School	Designer: Fernando Medina
8431	Banco Latino	Designer: Fernando Medina

8432 - 8456

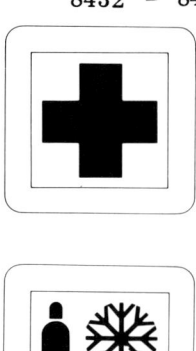 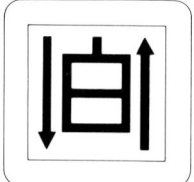   

8457

8458

8432-8456	Industrial Signs Designer: Dennis Ichiyama
8357	University anniversary mark Designer: Dennis Ichiyama
8358	The Monet Trio Designer: Dennis Ichiyama

Index of Marks and Designers

Aabagail Medical 7938
Acadia Landscaping 7437
Acapulco Gold Cup Race 7456
Acapulco Productions 7445
Acard Printing 7410
Accion Cultural y Asistencial . . 7866
Acciones y Valores de Mexico . 8354
Ackman-Yamomoto Opticians . 7936
Acorn Lodge, The 8101
Ad-Able Ltd. 7994
Adanac 8010
Ad-Centives West, Inc. 8208
Adega do Marques 7978
Administradora Tzocutumbac, S.A.
. . . . 8139
Administrative Studies 7631
Advance Signage 7881
AECIC 7989
Aerotopomex 7479
Africa S.A. 7645
Agencias Martin Loya 7461
Agriculture/Cattle Association . 7639
Agriculture & Energy 7718
Agriculture Production Technology,
Ltd. 7771
Aiea Optical 7933
Air Brake Specialists 8065
A.I. Freidman 8126
Aires del Mayab 7622
A.J. Wildman & Son, Inc. 7920
Alcohol Energy Company 7837
Alianza 8303
All American Sports Network . 7474
Allen Industrial Development
Statistics 7709
Allen Miller & Associates 7452
Allience for the Mentally Ill. . . 8063
Aloha State Realty 7934
Alta Tension 7462
Ambulatory Service 8455

American Back School 8396
American Bancorp 7526
American Express Company, learning
Resource Center 7917
American Federal Savings & Loan
. . . . 8380
American Graphics 8151
American Greeting Corporation. 7486
American Health Corporation, The
. . . . 8190
American Mining Congress . . . 8268
American ORT Federation . . . 7798
American Red Cross (Golden Spike
Division) 8221
American Scale Corporation . . 7802
Ameritrust 7514
AMF Harley-Davidson . . 8309, 8313
AMS, Inc. 8182
Amtrak 8073, 8083, 8085
Andres Garcia 7633
Ansbury Company, The 7393
Antonia Lowden Fiber Design. 8049
Aquarius, The 8417
Architectural Design Firm 8044
Arcuitur S.C. 7641
Arena Stage 8077
Argentina de Comercio 7867
Arie J. Geurts 7482
Aristos S.A. 7662
Arkansas Gazette 8088-8096
Arlene Hawkins Cosmetics . . . 8323
Arrow Maintenance Corp 8324
Art Council 7448
Arthritus Foundation (proposal)
. . . . 7735
Arthur Treacher's 7527
Ashland Beverage Center 8397
Associated Engineering Test
Laboratories 7434
Associated Rubber 7725

Associates in Physical Therapy. 8279
Associazione Indiastriali Varese
. . . . 7901
Astral Glass 7844
ATALAYA 7779
Atoms 8118
AT&T 8205
Audio Electronica de Mexico S.A.
. . . . 7659
Aurioles y Associates 7661
Aurora 8262
Aurora Plaza Hotel 7763
Auto Appraisers 8046
Auto Control 7780
Automated Hospital, The 7395
Avanti 8084
Avedos Zildjian Cymbal Company
. . . . 8272-8274
Avon Books 8189
Avondale Community Action . 8070
Avondale Swim & Tennis Club. 7721
Award 78 for the Greater Santa
Barbara Advertising Federation
. . . . 8242
Back to Basics, Home food
production and storage . . . 8036
Baja Inn Hotel 7438
Balseca 7600
Balseca S.A. 7595
Bananas 7985
Banco Aboumrad (suggested) . 7786
Banco Rural de Pesca 7634
Banco Latino 8431
Bancomer (proposal) 8024
Bandit Enterprizes 8297
Bank of California, The 7511
Banpesca 8304
Barbara Buckley 8023
Barclay Towers 7767
Barshop Enterprises 7879

Barton Investments, Inc.
.... 7760, 7765, & 7766
Baton Rouge Athletic & Racquet
   Club 7402
Beachside Resorts 7414
Bear Development Corp..... 7839
Beauty Supply 7467
Beeffalo (proposal) 7969
Beer Blanket for Leather Ltd.
   8241
Belmont Springs 8217
Bergquist Construction & Designs
   8237
Bettys Tours............. 7736
Bifano's................. 8055
Birnam Wood Golf Club..... 8246
Black Velvet Band, The 8013
Blackburn Productions...... 7424
Boar's Head Restaurant, Continental
   Restaurant System, Inc. . . 8233
Boats Inn................ 7703
Bob Banner and Associates ... 8115
Bob Collier Enterprises...... 8415
Bonin Realty 7773
Boom Restaurant 8426
Border Imports........... 7470
Botler Construction Co. 8413
Boutique Arlequin......... 7620
Boutique Vicky........... 7613
Bowling Club CPM........ 7666
Boyd Service, Inc. 8394
Brachet's Jazz Restaurant 7915
Breakers, The 7722
Bremen Elevator Co., Inc..... 7824
Brennan Construction Co., Inc. 8414
British Racing Motors....... 8125
Brock Hotel Corporation 7811-7815,
   . 7817-7819, 7821-7822, 7827-
   7835
Brock Real Estate Investment
   Corporation 7825
Brother Jacks 8011
Broward Federal Savings & Loan
   8383
Broward Mall 8198
Brown & Williamson International
   Tobacco 8255, 8260
Bryant Electronics......... 7739
B & S Glassworks 8258
Bub Bailey Construction..... 8038
Bub Shannon/Photography ... 7880
Buck.................. 7546
Budget Rent-a-Car......... 7531

Builder's Etc. 7398
Building Firm............ 8160
Bullard Realty 7734
Bullock, David and Nora, Graphic/
   Illustration........... 8067
Bumble + Bumble Hair Salon. . 7710
BVD Company, Union Underwear
   Co. 8197
Calafia Consultores 7441
Cal Cru 7670
California Association of Realtors
   8314
Callowhill Citizens Assoc., Inc.. 8069
Camellia Symphony Orchestra, The
   7961
Campbells de Mexico S.A..... 7607
Canas y Flores Producciones . . 7859
Capella choral group with Seed and
   Feed Theatre 8177
Cardamation............. 8146
Carder Company...... 8163-8164
Cardinal Federal Savings & Loan
   8377
Care Inns 8007
Carisma 8054
Carl Nelson, graphic designer. . 8181
Carlson, Inc.............. 7757
Carlton, The............. 7945
Carnabi 7561
Carolina Truck Center, Inc.... 7951
Carousel 7519
Carsa.................. 7535
Carter Seeds............. 8235
Carton y Papel de Mexico S.A.
   .... 7625, 7585
Carton y Papel ole Mexico S.A.
   7573
Casa dos Presentes......... 7980
Casa Rosos S.A. 7663
Casey Jones Bar 8240
Cassano Enterprises 7509
Casual Kut........... 8154, 8168
Catholic Charity Committee . . 7698
Caustic Material 8439
Cavas Bach S.A. 7591
CDQ Printing 8156
Cemento Atoyac 7541
Cemento Campana......... 7539
Cemento Centenario 7542
Cementos Tolteca 7533
Cemento Victoria 7540
Central Florida Multi Housing
   Association 8280

Central Studio 7998
Centro de Arte Fic......... 7860
Centro de Desarrollo de Personal
   8356
Cereales Industrializados S.A... 7611
Certified Pool Corp......... 8223
CFC Group, The 7882
Chaney & Associates 7740
Charles Restaurant......... 8257
Charlotte Motor Speedway ... 7948
The Charlotte Nature Museum . 7953
Charlotte Potts........... 8005
Charlotte Speech & Hearing Center
   7949
Cheapskates 8267
Chiclet Adams de Mexico S.A.. 7603
Chicory Hills Development ... 8068
Children in America exhibit, symbol
   for 8175
Choice in Therapy, A....... 7923
Cia. Abille, S.A. 7432
Cigarrera la Moderna 7605
Cineautos Nacionales C.A..... 8141
Circulation Tools, Inc........ 8247
City Center 8379
Ciudad Obrego'n.......... 8027
Clamex 7473
Clarion Car Radios......... 7560
Clark Gas............... 8382
Clarken Enterprises 7973
Clearwater Village 8113
Clinica Anchieta 7979
Coast Village Plaza......... 8051
Codi 7545
Cody.................. 7406
Coffee Company 7962
Coffee House, The (East Texas State
   Univ.) 8287
Coleccion Marke 7583
Collegio de Bachilleres 7635
College for architects 7637
Colorado Business Telephone. . 7397
Columbus Day 7404
Comercial Mexicana S.A. 7599
Comision Latinamericana de
   Administracion para el
   Desarrollo 8140
Command Travel Inc........ 7922
Commons at Mendham...... 8100
Communicateurs Assucies 7905
Community Self-Reliance Center,
   The................ 8075
Communique 8147

Complejo Habitacional "Bristol Center" 7858
Comsemar, S.A. 8302
Condominium Concepts 8229
Concord Properties 8004
"Conmaeca". 7566
Connecticut Off-Track Betting. 8196
Consolidated Amusement 7941
Constranza Geurts 7484
Construction Company . . 7567, 8045
Constructora Tabares 8026
Construis 7790
Corematica-Computing Division 8398
Corematica-Consulting in Administration Division . . 8399
Corporate Programming Inc. . . 7794
Cornell University 8076
Corporacion de Turismu de Venezuela 8143
Corner Boys, The 8216
Costa Coffee 8358
Costa Palma 7468
Country Store, The 7729
CPM 7576
CPM, Christmas theme . . 7615, 7627
Creativity and Design 7654
Croix Media Communications . 7972
Crown Toyota 8230
Crusader Equipment Inc. 7741
CS Enterprises (proposal) 8224
CSC Properties 7876
Cuenca & Associates 7959
Custom Collison 8014
Danger to Life 8449
Dapco Industries 8346
Darien Connecticut Indian Guides 7525
Daryl Cushenbery 7808
David Butler Company 7963
David Osborne 8392
Dawn Marie Skin Care Center . 7930
DeAvedon & Co. 8310
Deciduous Press, The 8059
Del Guercio, Inc., R. 8110
Delta Express 8429
Deneal's 7420
Denver Triathon, The 7392
Desarrollos Arquitecturas Maritimos 7469
Designer Craftsmen 7435
Designer siminar (Mexico), theme for 7643

Designcore de Mexico. 7444
Designers Logotype (Steven Skaggs) 8173
Diana Garcia and Associates . . 7429
Digital Associates 7510
Digital Eqipment Corporation . 8271
Diners Club International 7493
Diostigre 7449
Dipak, S.A. 7428
Dirt 8123
Discount King. 7891
Display International S.A. 7653
Distribuidora Atoto, S.A. 7433
Dixie 5 7708
Do Not Touch 8454
DOD. 7562
Don Connelly 7742
Doneketesen, The 8056
Dorchester Corporation 8389
Downtown Business Services, Inc. 8410
DPI Labs 7407
Dr. Linda C. Gardner 7673
Drum Corps International/Montreal 1981 7401
Duraclean S.A. 7642
Dusal Instrument Corp. 7793
Eagle Mobile Homes & Campers 7706
Ear protection 8455
Earth Resources Company . . . 8284
Eastridge Mall. 8200
Ebesa 7604, 7617
Econafta 7864
Editorial Grijalbo: Simbolo de la Portada "Los Sentidos Al Aire" 7870
Edwin M. Rollins, Inc. 7687
EJF Graphic Design 8268
E.J. Wolf 8202
Electrica Hernandez. 7668
Electrica Montevideo 7669
Electrol, S.A. 8128
Elizabethtown City Schools. . . 8256
Elizabethtown, Ky. 8259
Emerson/Nichols/Bailey 7823
Emmanuel Carambola Grove . . 8321
Empire State Convention Center 7896
Employment development . . . 7579
Emyco S.A. 7552
Encinitos Office Building 7887
Encuentro 7784

English Montessori School, The 8430
Ernesto Coco Transportes 7862
Erwin Schwarz Jeweler. 7848
Equity, Inc. 7682
Estilo 7782
Explosive material. 8434
Express Repair Service 7421
Eve Communication Service, Inc. 7674
Eze Brew Coffee Service 8403
Facial respirator 8441
Family Couseling Center. 7699
Febca 7439
Fermex S.A. 7646
Fernando Bustos, trusteeship. . 7789
Fieldstone 8149
Fidelity Federal Savings and Loan 7528
Filteration Systems, Inc. 8248
Fire extinguisher 8442
First National Bank of Yorktown 7883
First Union National Bank ... 7518
Flammable material 8445
Fleetwood Cartage. 7693
Fleetwood Enterprises Inc. . . . 7492
Flexnit Co., Inc. 8206
Flor 7791
Florasia (Rock Group) 7810
Florence Crittenton Services . . 7691
F.L. Russell Corp. 8021
F.L. Stephens 8161
Fork lift 8448
Foothill Solar Exchange 7841
Foulger-Okland Company . . . 8409
Fox River Paper Company ... 8311
Franklin State Bank. 8112
Free Bus-Victoria City Hall ... 8408
Friendly Ice Cream Corporation 7487
Frisco Electronics 8210
FPR, Inc. 8395
F. Terry Callahan, attorney and counselor at law 8003
Fundacion Mexicana Para el Descarrollo Rural 7785
Furniture Represenative. 8042
Galleria Arte Borgogna. 7910
Gallery Kashahare 7995
Gamesa S.A. 7485
Garcia Architects. 8052

Garden Gate Restaurant 8218
Gatty Communications, Inc. . . 8079
George Edmonston Jr. 7419
Georgia Bankers Association . . 7754
Georgia General Soccer (proposal)
. . . . 7726
Georgia Heart Association "Lifeline"
. . . . 7753
Georgia Hospital Association . . 8176
Gerotours 7460
Globe Tel Aviv-Travel Service Ltd.
. . . . 8253
G & G Specialties 8087
Gift Shop at the High Museum of
Art, Atlanta 8178
Gillmore & Right Co. 7702
Giraf Grafix 8071
GLCS Bar 7783
Glacier Raft Company 8227
G.M. Hogshead Co. 7689
Goffstein, Gaston, & Nakash . . 7476
Goodies by Gourmet 7872
Goulet Dental Laboratory 8344
Granada Hills Community Hospital-
Children's Services 8317
Grand Central Racqueball Club
. . . . 7918
Graphic Impressions 8167
Graphis 7787
Grat Atlantic & Pacific Tea
Company, The 7517
Great Basin Realty 8209
Great Foot Race, The 7399
Great South East Music Hall
Emporium & Performing Arts
Exchange, Inc., The 8185
Greenberg and Greenberg Architects
. . . . 7391
Greenpeace 7937
Grupo Baja Muk 8028
Grupo Castell S.A. 7632
Grupo Cinco 7440
Grupo Cuatro 8029
Grupo Domit 8353
GTR Wallcovering Co. . . 8015-8017
Guaranty Bank 7396
Gucker & Goldstein Inc. 8186
Guia Civil Qi 7854
Gulf Coast Supply 7408
Guma Footwear, Ltd. 8022
Habana Park Condominiums . . 8281
Haena Shoes 7939
Haley-Roth Medical Equipment, Inc.
. . . . 7394
Hallenberger & Associates Consulting
Engineers 7886
Hallmark Institute 8294
Halls Department Store . 8361-8376
Handweaver's Guild of America, Inc.
. . . . 7970
Harcourt-Brace-Johanovich . . . 7447
Harmony Classics, Inc. 7719
Harris Teeter Supermarkets . . . 7500
Harwell Enterprises 7950
Hayashida Ltd. 7997
Health Maintenance Center . . . 8191
Helados Balam 8357
Henred Trailers 7574
Hidden Meadow Apartments . . 8002
High voltage 8450
Hilton Head Company, The . . . 7947
Hirt Realty 7746
Holder Well Company 7733
Home National Bank 8393
Honey s.r.l. 7904
Hospice of Schenectady 7894
Hospital Santelena 8348
Housing Coalition, The 7932
Housing Management Ltd. 8078
HP Enterprises 8225
Huebner & Henneberg, Architects
. . . . 7892
Hungry Mouth 8119
Hunt, Leuchars, & Hepburn Ltd.
. . . . 7563
Hypnosis Training Institute . . . 7916
I Congreso Latinoamericano de
Neurocirugia 8142
ICSID, XI Congres of industrial
design, Mexico 7644
IDS Tax-Empt Bond Fund . . . 8171
Ibex Pension Actuaries Inc. . . . 7796
Ice Cream Parlor 7609
Ideal Fastener Corp. 8266
Ignacio Villareal 7577
Imco Precision Products Inc. . . 7807
Imed Corporation 8116
Impex International Corporation
. . . . 7430
Incataba 7602
Incubadora Cajeme, S.C. 8133
Indian Fetish, Indian jewelry . . 8162
Industrial de Alimentos 7608
Industrial elevator 8437
Industrial scale 8452
Industrial signs 8432-8458
Industrializadora de cacao de
Tabasco S.A. 7582
Information/security officer . . 8438
Institute for Advanced Studies . 7597
Institute for the Study of Human
Knowledge, Inc. 7804
Interchoice Contracting 7902
Interface Educational Consultants
. . . . 7776
Interior Design 7697
International Aerosol Seminar . 7616
International Women's Writing Guild
. . . . 7924
InverMexico 8351
Investment Properties Group, The
. . . . 7530
Isseks Brothers, Inc. 8194
Ireco Chemicals 8222
Jack Okland, Jr./designer 8418
Jackson County Family Life Council
. . . . 8060
Janet, toy manufacturers 7589
Japan Ad-Art, Inc. 7992
Jardines de Chapultepec 7463
Jardines de la Mesa 7459
Jean Store, The 7846
JeansWest 8400
JeSuis Unisex Salon 8343
Jewish Sports Club, Mexico . . . 7570
JFSA 8001
J.L. Marrow Lithographers . . . 8327
J.L. Owens & Company 7849
Jo, artist 8155
John Allphin 7426
John E. King Tax Consultant . . 8238
John K. Landis Graphic Design
. . . . 8040
John W. Clark Oil 8381
Jorge Canales & Associates . . . 8301
Johan Inc. 7521
Jose Garcia Luna 7788
Journal of Reading 7752
Julian Alvarez, illustrator 8401
J & W Aircraft Maintenance . . 8277
J.W. Sayles & Associates 8285
Kach All 8386
Kagan Associates, Inc., Paul . . . 7803
Kappa Corp. 8214
Kayser-Roth Hosiery Co., Inc.—
No Nonsense 8201
K & B Drugs 7498
Keep under cool temperature . . 8433
Keil Investment Brokers 7442
Kellogs de Mexico S.A. 7592
Kent Typographic Service 8265
Kentucky Farmers Bank 8390
KGRC Radio Station 7890
Khaki's 7676
Kimm's Trading Company 7415

Kissin' Her Pub 8145
K-Sweet Radio 7820
L. Fernandez 7557
L. Rosen Productions 8106
La Campana S.A. 7584
La Pelicula 7855
La Quinta Motor Inns, Inc. . . . 8295
Laboratorio de Diseno y Analisis de
   Mercado 7481
Ladrillera Monterrey, S.A. 7532
Lake Park Gardens 8289
Lamarco Insurance 8252
Lamport Co., The 8263
Lance S.A. 7558
Landmark Advertising Incorporated
   8009
Landscape Design 7675
Langeman & Cape 7559
Larkin Coils 7732
Larry Alexander Advertising . . 7575
Las Conchas 7618
Laurel Hill 8109
LDS Church 8219
LDS, Inc. 8008
Leadership Resources Inc. 7494
Leaf 'n Petal 7955
Learning Store Ltd., The 7926
LeeAnn Brook Design 7837
Leif Hope's Laundry Restaurant
   7921
Len Bannister Advertising 7700
l'Erbolario 7907-7908
Let Bygones Be!—Antiques . . . 8264
Lincoln Financial Corporation
   7927
Lincoln Theater, The 7704
Linda Prusse—Creative Services
   8207
Little Apple Corporation, The . 8359
Littlefield Publishing Company, Inc.
   8282
Living Quarters, Inc. 8086
Loading/unloading. 8435
Lodge Apartments, The 7884
Logotipo de la Obra de Teatro:
   "Woyzeck" 7869
Lopez Guerra Arquitectos, S.C. 8130
Lora Boylan, Interior Design . . 7968
Lorraine Press (proposal) 8228
Love & Dugger 7873
Luby Enterprises 7758
Luis Olvera, designer 7660
Lyon Moving & Storage 7496

McCullough & Sons Welldrilling . 7991
M. Domit 8352
Magna IX 7409
Magic Carpet, The 7852
Magnum Transportation 7929
Mammouth Mountain Lodge . . 7692
Mammut Costruzioni 7911
Man & Universe 7580
Manifattura Naj-Oleari 7900
Maracaju Veiculos 7977
Mario Eskenazi, graphic designer
   8402
Mario Monti Editore 7912
Market Data Associates 7684
Marketing by Design, Inc. 7965
Marlene Glasser Public Relations &
   Advertising 7878
Marli-bras 7983
Martex 7457
Master Broker Associates 8276
Master Marketing Group 7513
Materias Primas Monterrey S.A. . 7861
Matthews Real Estate Company
   7761
Medical aid 8432
Medical Economics Co. 8103
Medical Properties 8006
Meisel Photochrome Corp. . . . 8293
Melville Shoe 7523, 7529
Memorial Hospital of Panorama City
   8316
Merchadise House 7416
Merrill Lynch Property Development
   8254
Metrocraft Publishing 7750
Metropolitan Life Insurance
   Company 8334-8340
Metropolitan Transit Authority
   7711
Mexico City sports promotion . 7628
Mexican Association of Bakers . 7640
Mexican Citrus Growers Association
   7664
Mexican Finance Executives
   Association 7626
Mexican Institute of Finance
   Executives 7586
Mexican Lemon Growers Association
   7665
Mexican Ministry of Finance
   . . . . 7630, 7658
Mexican Paper Association . . . 7587
Mexican Paper/Cellulose Seminar
   7569

Mexican Tourism theme 7638
Mid-America Dance Company,
   Wichita State University . . . 8030
Milwaukee Metropolitan Sewage
   District 8331
Mini Mail Boxes 7888
Minnesota Automobile Dealers
   Association, The 8097
Minnesota Orchestral Association
   75th symbol 8172
Mino Films 8428
Miran-Marcas 7981
Mission Chemical 8236
Mobay Chemical 7522
Modular Movers 7743
Moldes Industriales 8347
Monet Trio, The 8458
Monogram or symbol for the name
   Joy 8064
Monroe Enquirer Journal 7680
Moore Electric Supply, Inc. . . . 7677
Moores Department Store (proposal)
   7735
Morishita Co., Ltd. 7999
Morris & Associates Realtors . . 7690
Mountain Wool & Weaving Supply
   Company 7851
Movenpik 7489
M-R Studios 8058
Mr. & Mrs. Geurts 7483
MTC 7443
Muebles Norden S.A. 7593
Multhipla 7909
Multi-Press 7903
Musidora Films 8427
National Association of Counties
   8081
National Consumer Finance
   Association 7502
National Graphics 7728
National Horse Show 7455
National Hotel 7838
National Institute for the Psycho-
   therapies, Inc. 7806
National Shirt Shops 8193
Nevada Balloon Club 7705
Nevada County Arts Council . . 7843
Nevada County Aviation 7840
Nevada County Legal Assistance, Inc.
   7842
Nevada Council on the Arts . . . 8050
New Approach Method 8420

New England Association for Hospital Development 7503
New Market Business Park. . . . 7755
New World Learning System—Educational Kits 8406
New York City, Department of Parks and Recreation 7913
New York Pasta Co., The 8416
New York State Cooperative Extensive. 8080
News. 7453
Niel Schiller 8016
Nino Lo Duca. 7906
No Smoking. 8453
North Country Store Works. . . 8031
Northridge Mall. 8204
Norwalk Montessori Association 7491
Nova Art Consultants. 8179
NOVUM Gebrauchsgrafik 7547
Nuevo Centro Urbano 7446
Nurion 8150
Occasions. 7400
Ocean Flesh 8322
Ocean Garden Products, Inc. . . 8234
Oil Field 8251
Okray's 8192
Old Orchard Shopping Center . 8061
Olin and Wilson, Accountants . 7960
One Eyed Tomcat, Inc.. 7952
Orduno, emplement service. . . 7581
Organizational services Inc. . . . 7738
Ornelas S.A. 7612
Ortho Pharmaceuticals 7490
OTEARCA (Compania Constructora) 8144
Outsiders for Leather Ltd.. . . . 8239
Oxbow Ranch. 7497
Paddy Wack Apparel 8291
Paintwell Co. 7893
Palm. 7572
Palmas del Mar 8153
Palms, The 7724
Palomar Legal Services 7477
Panam S.A. 7606
Paper and Cellulose Association. 7667
Paracom, Inc. 7713
Paradise Found 7694
Parera S.A. 7594
Pariscope Design 8419, 8421
Parke Institute 8165
Parker Chemicals. 7413

Parkville Water Works. 7425
Parque Reforma 8350
Parts Depot 8388
Pasquale Food Company. 7501
Pat Olson. 8249
Paul Kagan Associates, Inc. . . . 7799
Pearlridge Mall 8187
Pencil Point Graphic Adv. 8286
Pennington Design. 8074
Perforadora Mexico, S.A. 8131
Perfusion Service, Inc. 8341
Peter R. Paterson. 8018
Peterson-Gasser & Assoc. 8226
Penta 7466
Philadelphia Area Newsletter. . 8170
Pickett-Rotholz and Murphy . . 7967
Pic 'n Pay Shoes, Inc. 7954
Piktor's Metamorphosis, Inc. . . 8122
Pinellas Apartments Association 8278
Pioneer Products 8158
Place, The 8012
Plan West 7770
Plasticos Impala, S.A. 7431
Plaza Bosques 8349
Plaza Camino Real/Mission Valley Center. 7451
Plaza Properties. 8378
Pocket Billiards, Red Scholefield 8034
Ponto de Encontro 7987
Ponys 7471
Posto Jumbo 7976
Potros 7472
Practical Sciences, Inc. 7774
Practitioners Forum 7749
Preakness Gourmet Deli 8111
Preconcreto 7536
Premesa 7537
Primer Concurso Nacional de Diseno y Fabricacion Mobiliario de Interes Socail 7857
Private Book Collection 7506
Procalsa 7544
Producciones Del Plata 7863
Productos Congelados S.A. . . . 7598
Productos Sahler 7556
Profamilia S.A. 7578
Professional Theatre Program. . 8345
Prografic 8424
Progressive Grocer Company . . 7919
Promont 7478

Protective face shield 8446
Protor. 7781
Purpera & Sons Home Center. . 7422
Quali-T Automotive. 8104
Quigley 8124
Radio Cidade 7974
Radio Station project. . . 7553, 7554
Radioactive material 8444
Rainbow Camera. 7928
Rainbow Rentals. 8215
Ramada Inn-Coliseum . 7672, 7678, 7679, 7683, 7686
Ratterree Knife Company, Inc. 7685
Realist, Inc.. 8308
Reconstruction Inc. 7745
Red Cross-Metro Atlanta. 7737
Reitsport Ruhm 7996
Reno International Airport . . . 8048
Research Group, The 7403
Restaurante Califia 7454
Reynolds Asphalt Paving. 7744
R.F. Tophovan 7568
R.H. Johnson Company 7488
R.H. Swenarton Associates . . . 8342
Ricardo's Mexican Restaurant 7610, 7621
Rimsky Enterprises, Inc.. 7671
Roberto Dosil. 8405
Robinson Excavating 8384
Rochester Steel. 7707
Rockhill Cencert Ballet Co.. . . 7681
Rockwell International, North American Space Operations Employees Action Circle. . 7772
Rodex S.A. 7590
Rollroma. 8025
Romance for Two 8423
"Root" 7636
Rosenstein's Jewels 7874
Rotary Specialties, Inc.. 8250
Roxborough Park Development Corporation 7756
Roxbury Publishing Co. 7480
Roy White's Flowers 7946
Royal Axman, Inc., The 7716
Royale 7464
S.A. Railways. 7565
Sacramento Film Festival 7966
Sacsa. 7538
SafeCo. Insurance 7524
Safety Floaters for Leather Ltd. 8245

Safety helmet............ 8451	Skeptic 7990	Suburbon Electronics... 7897-7899
Safety goggles............ 8436	Sketch............... 7986	Sullivant Rush Cross Realty, Inc.
Safrex tools 7571	Ski Togs Sportswear......... 7712	 7411
Sahitur, Tabasco .. 8129, 8136-8138	Skin Cancer Foundation, The . 7792	Sunbelt 7731
Sails, The............. 7730	Skylight Productions 8319	Sun International Inc........ 8232
III Salon de Escultura y Obra Grafica	Smith-Scharff............ 7720	Sun Pacific Properties....... 8244
.... 7853	Snugglers' Hearth, Vermont... 8102	Sun Ray Products, Inc....... 7701
Salon de Gout............ 8000	Sofico Vacaciones......... 8425	Sunshine Unlimited Solar Systems
Sal's Pizzaroma........... 8066	Software International, S.A. .. 8132	 7475
San Jan Pools Inc........... 7875	Solar Development Company.. 7942	Suntech Construction....... 7850
San Jemo............. 7614	Solar Energy, group for 7418	Sunward Investments, Inc. ... 8283
San Pedro Peninsula Hospital.. 8315	Solarmex............. 7464	Surf Tours 7935
Santa Barbara Design/Build	Soifer Cristales Templados ... 7856	Suspended load............ 8440
Incorporated 8057	Solector............. 7865	SYCOM, Inc............ 8183
Santa Cruz Community Credit Union	Sound Column Productions... 8035	Systems Associates, Inc...... 7956
.... 7958	"The Sound of Children" 8320	Tana Corporation 7759
Santiago Textil, S.A......... 8307	Southend Development 7512	Target Promotion Inc........ 8328
Saratoga Performing Arts Center,	Southern California Department of	Tecate................ 7436
Inc.............. 8203	Water and Power....... 8114	Technical & Marketing Services Corp.
Saw Service 8043	Space Techniques, Inc....... 7688	 8298
Scripps Clinic and Research	Specialty Graphics......... 7723	Technition Group, The...... 8195
Foundation 8121	Spectra-Media Communications	Tecnofon Comunicaciones ... 7868
Seabreeze............. 7417	 7555	Tell Tale Sales............ 8261
Seagull Communications..... 7423	SpectraVision............ 7877	Temple Emanual.......... 8296
Sears Roebuck de Mexico S.A.. 7655	Spencer Group, The........ 7696	Tenis del Valle, S.A......... 8305
Searle White Knight Textiles .. 8312	Spies................ 7564	Tenth House Enterprises Inc... 7925
Second Cousin Restaurant.... 7717	Sports MetaSkills.......... 7515	Teradyne.............. 8270
Security Benefit Group of	Springdale 8105	Terra Cotta 8422
Companies......... 7816	Stanley Drugs........... 7751	Terra Craft for Terra Craft Corp.
Selective Marketing Service Group	Starfire 8148	 8243
.... 8325	State of Colorado/Litter Control	Terri Mesiti Graphic Design... 8332
Sell your Own Home 8039	Program............ 7768	Thalians Community Mental Health
Seminar for secretaries 7657	State of Mexico, archives 7647	Center at Cedars-Sinai Medical
Seminars on Success........ 8220	State of Mexico, board room.. 7650	Center............. 8318
Senar 7975	State of Mexico, cleaning 7652	Thomas Snowdon Associates, Inc.
Servicios Profesionales 7534	State of Mexico, planning 7651	 8411
Servicios Turisticos 7458	State of Mexico, reception ... 7649	Thorton Hubburd School of
S. Grimaldi............ 8108	State of Mexico, waiting room. 7648	Mixology........... 8330
Shear Sensations......... 7971	Staten Island Children's Museum	Three Bears, ice cream parlor.. 8152
S.H.C.P............... 7656	 8180	Thrushwood Realty........ 7507
Sheraton Maui Hotel 7940	Steppin' Out............ 8120	Tiger Club, Auburn University. 8033
Sherlock Holmes (proposal)... 8032	Stingers-Salt Lake City Pro	Tilysa 8135
Shipyard Plantation........ 7957	Volleyball 8211	Time Center Jewelers 7895
Sierra Nevada Museum of Art . 8047	Store room desk 8443	Time clock.............. 8447
Sierra Timberline.......... 7847	Stormont—Vail Regional Medical	Tipiti 7982
Sierra Water Systems 7845	Center............ 7809	Tomlinson Engineering Company
Sigma Phi Epsilon National	Strike One 8169	 7944
Fraternity 7871	Strome Inc.............. 8174	Topper Toys Corp.......... 8326
Sikorsky 7505	Structural Systems......... 8037	Tourist development ... 7588, 7619
Sisk Company Inc., The . 8098-8099	Struthers Electronics Corp.... 7795	Toyota Dealers Assn.... 8212-8213
Sistema Urbano de Tracao Electrica	Student Activity Board (East Texas	Tracsa................ 8300
.... 7988	State University)....... 8288	Traffic Associates 8062
Six Flags over Texas.... 8292, 8299	Studio Film & Tape Inc...... 7805	Trans-America Corp......... 8072

Transmar.................7543
Transportes Kinematos, S.A. de C.V.
.................8134
Tri-Medical...............8391
Tri-Seal International Inc.....7801
Trinity College...........7495
Trust Conference..........7748
12 Week Diet Club.........8385
Twin Anchors Marine.......7695
Type Factory, The.........8166
Typographic Images Inc......7800
Unger Construction Company.7964
Ultramag.................8355
Unica, S.A...............8306
Unigraphics Corporation.....7427
United, financial institution...7551
United Neighborhood House of N.Y.
.................8329
United States Employment Service,
    U.S. Department of Labor. 7504
United Van Lines..........7499
United Wire Hanger........8107
Unitika Berkshire Co., Ltd....7993
Univac Div. of Sperry Rand...7797
Universidad Femenina de Mexico
.................7778
University Anniversary Mark..8457
Unversity of British Columbia
    International Intervisitation
    Program.............8407
Unpublished (waterbeds)....8290
Uptown Eddie's Restaurant...7715
U.S. Sanitary.............7596
Valumed..................7450
Van Nuys Travel Agencies....8041
Venture Foods, Incorporated..8188
VIDEA- Victoria International
    Development Educational
    Association..........8404
Video Record Services......7727
Viewpoint Associates.......7762
Vila Camoes..............7984
Village Square Condominiums. 8275
Vintage Cars..............7931
Vivian S. Haas/Illustrator....8412
Volume Shoe Corporation
.... .7508, 7520, 7576
Voyager..................8117
WAMX...................8387
WBTV/Jefferson-Pilot Broadcasting
    Co..................7943
Watch Works, The.........8127

Wearhouse, The...........8082
Wel-Don Appliance Service...8333
Western Crude Oil, Inc......7764
Westpac Interiors..........8053
Whispering Oaks Apartments..7885
Whittier Hills Baptist Church..7775
"The Whole Shootin' Match"..8184
Why Weight, Jesse S. Miller, Ph. D. &
    Jacqueline A. Smith, Ph. D.
.................7914
Wicker Works Video Productions
.................7769
Wild Strawberries.........8360
Wilson S.A...............7601
Windsor Plaza Shopping Center
.................7889
Wood & Wong............8020
Woodfield Mall...........8199
Woodmeyer..............7412
World Invitational Tournament
.................7714
World Wide Locations......7405
Yankee Sawyer............7777
Zeigler Engineering Sales, Inc..8231

Ahbe, Susan M.; Saba Design Inc., 12 Charles Lake Road, North Oaks, MN 55110

Allen, Chuck; Pencil Point, 13740 Midway Road, Suite 504, Dallas, TX 75234

Allen, Steve; 88 Andros Road, Palm Springs, FL 33461

Alexander, John M.; Graphic Design/Advertising, 330 East Canon Perdido, Santa Barbara, CA 93101

Alexander Jr., Theodore; 6283 N. Cicero Ave., Chicago, IL 60646

Ambrosino, Thomas J.; Ambrosino Design Group, Rt. 55 Grahamsville, NY 12740

Anglim, John R.; The Sisk Company Inc., 2001 Beach Street, Fort Worth, TX 76103

Asher, Connie; Graphic Design, 915 Steele, Denver, CO 80206

Austin, Patrick; Patrick Austin Graphics, 10942 Wye Drive, Suite 200, San Antonio, TX 78217

Aveles, Anthony; Harper + George Inc., 307 East 47 Street, New York, NY

Baden, Carl; Matrix Design Inc., 360 South Monroe, Suite 310, Denver, CO 80209

Banaim, Ricardo; Apartado 70.103 Los Ruices, Caracas 2.p. 107, Venezuela

Baptista, Ted; TEDesign, 3577-5 Pinao Street Honolulu, HI 96822

Baronet, William; C. Scott & Co., 315 St. Landry St., Lafayette, LA 70506

Bohon, Ed; Ed Bohon Graphic Design, 43-23 Colden Street, Flushing, NY 11355

Brook, LeeAnn; Miners Village, 206 Sacramento Street, Suite 306, Nevada City, CA 95959

Bullock, David; David & Nora Bullock, graphic design/illustration, 617 Luella Drive, Kutztown, PA 19530

Cairns, Julie Ann; Children's Hospital and Health Center, staff artist, 8001 Frost Street, San Diego, Ca 92123

Carter, Dave; David E. Carter Corporate Communications, Inc., 1505 Carter Ave., P.O. Box 591, Ashland, KY 41101

Canales, Jorge; Vicente Garcia Torres, 149 3 Coyoacan, Mexico 21, D.F.

Cline, Clint; Littlefield Publishing Company, 5401 W. Kennedy Blvd., Suite 222, Tampa, FL 33609

Colin, Sergio; Laboratorio de Diseno y Analisis de Mercado, S.A. Reforma 185 8º Piso Mexico 5, D.F.

Congdon, Arthur S.; Congdon Macdonald Inc., 420 Lexington Avenue, New York, NY 10170, also Lippincott & Margulies, Inc.

Contrefas, Mucio; Laboratorio de Diseno y Analisis de Mexicado, S.A. Reforma 185 8º Piso Mexico 5, D.F.

Connelly, Don; Don Connelly & Associates, P.O. Box 536, 108 N. Avondale Rd., Avondale Estates, GA 30002

Cushenbery, Daryl; Emerson/Nichols/Bailey Inc., 1117 Merchants National Bank Building, Topeka, KS 66612

Deiter, Su; Emerson/Nichols/Bailey Inc., 1117 Merchants National Bank Building, Topeka, KS 66612

DeSieno, John; Madison North Ltd., 17 Fairlawn Ave., Albany, NY 12203

Diseno, S.C., Morfos; Ignacio Esteva 24, San Miguel Chapultepec, Mexico 18, D.F.

Donahey, Trish; 27 East Central Avenue, C-2, Paoli, PA 19301

Edwards, Graham; Laboratorio de Diseno y Analisis de Mercado S.A. Reforma 185 8º Piso Mexico 5, D.F.

Eckel, Len; Len's Visual Design, P.O. Box 8308, Missoula, MT 59807

Eckstein & Associates Inc., Arthur; 415 Lexington Avenue, New York, NY 10017

Flanagan, Ed; Mike Quon/Graphic Design, 53 Spring Street, New York, NY 10012

Forstenzer, Ellen J.; Ellen June Forstenzer/creative design, 145 East 16th Street, New York, NY 10003

Fritz-Zavacki, Ron; Marketing by Design Inc., 716 Alhambra Blvd., Sacramento, CA 95816

Garcia-Luna, Jose A.; Isla Magdalena N 75 Col. Prado Vallejo Tlalnepantla, Edo. de Mexico

Gersin Associates, Robert P.; Industrial Design, 11E 22nd Street, New York, NY 10010

Geurts, Arie J.; Laboratorio de Diseno y Analisis de Mercado, Carton y Papel de Mexico, S.A., Reforma 185 8º Piso, Mexico 5, D.F.

Graham, Thomas J.; Calligraphics, Inc., 521 West Ormsby Ave., Louisville, KY 40203

Grimaldi, Stephanie; Gero & Bierstein Inc., 190 Moore Street, Hackensack, NJ 07601

Grupo Cuatro; Manuel M. Ponce 255 Mexico, 20 d.f.

Gutierrez, Fco.; Laboratorio de Diseno y Analisis de Mercado S.A. Reforma 185 8º Piso Mexico 5, D.F.

Gutke, Gordon; Gordon Gutke and Associates Advertising Art, Suite 200 Metropolitan Plaza, 2480 South Main, Salt Lake City, UT 84115

Hart Communications, 7129 Waterman Ave., St. Louis, MO 63130

Heaton, Kevin; Croix Media Communications, 726 So. 7th Street, Stillwater, MN 55082

Henderson, Richard D.; 4173 Chartley Drive, Bridgeton, MO 63044

Honda, Alex; Laboratorio de Diseno y Analisis de Mercado S.A. Reforma 185 8º Piso Mexico 5, D.F.

HumanGraphic, 3329 First Ave., San Diego, CA 92103

Ichiyama, Dennis; 9000 E. Lincoln Road, Apt. 1609, Wichita, KS 67207

Ikola, Gale William; Gale William and Associates, 6100 Golden Valley Road, Minneapolis, MN 55422

Korves, Douglas, Harper + George Inc., 307 East 47 Street, New York, NY

Kridel, Tim; Matrix Design Inc., 360 South Monroe, Suite 310, Denver, CO 80209

Larson, Ken; 3047 North Cramer Street, Milwaukee, WI 53211

Latocki, William A.; Advergraphics, Ltd., 1935 Pauline Boulevard, Parline Plaza, Suite 100-13, Ann Arbor, MI 48103

Leidel, Michael B.; 259 G. Street S.W. Washington, D.C. 20024

Litten, Reginald K.; Sugarcreek Concepts, 221 Greenmount Boulevard, Dayton, OH 45419

Lizotte, David A.; Gunn Associates, 275 Newbury Street, Boston, MA 02116

Locke, Larry; 470 Cherry Apt. 6, Long Beach, CA 90802

Lyerly, Elaine M.; Eve Communication Services, Inc., One Charlottetown Center Suite 133, Charlotte, NC 28204

Maude, Cindy; Emerson/Nichols/Bailey Inc., 1117 Merchants National Bank Building, Topeka, KS 66612

McDougal, Lauren S.; 1851 Columbia Rd. N.W., Apt. 209, Washington, DC 20009

Medina, Fay; Laboratorio de Diseno y Analisis de Mercado S.A. Reforma 185 8o Piso Mexico 5, D.F.

Medina, Fernando; Santiago Bernabeu, 6 Madrid

Mesiti, Terri; 137 Oakland Ave., Methuen, MA 01844

Miller, Allan; Allan Miller & Associates, 614 Fifth Ave., Suite C, San Diego, CA 92101

Miranda, Oswaldo; Aristoxenes Bittencourt, 297, (Taruma), Curitiba/Parana/Brazil, C=P 80.000

Morris, C. Spencer; Arkansas Gazette, P.O. Box 1821, Little Rock, AR 72203

Nelson, Carl; 13945 Holley Rd., Eden Prairie, MN 55344

Oishi, Masahiro; Japan Ad-Art, Inc., 1-25-403, Dojima 2-shome, Kita-Ku, Osaka 530 Japan

Okland Jr., Jack; P.O. Box 15448, Salt Lake City, UT 84115

Olvera, Luis; Laboratorio de Diseno y Analisis de Mercado S.A. Reforma 185 8o Piso Mexico 5, D.F.

Palam, James F.; Palam Design, graphic design/advertising, 330a East Canon Perdido Santa Barbara, CA 93101

Paris Jr., Isaac; Pariscope Design, 349 E. 14th St., rm. 4r, New York, NY 10009

Peeri, Ilan; 3 Cremieux St., Tel-Aviv Tl. (03) 227703

Pellicone, John; Box 42 A, Ga. Rd., Franklin, NC

Potts, Charlotte; 15103 Elm Park, San Antonio, TX 78247

Powers, Mike; The Blackburn Company Inc., 2322 Tremont Dr., Suite 102, Baton Rouge, LA 70809

Prus, Wanda; Emerson/Nichols/Bailey Inc., 1117 Merchants National Bank Building, Topeka, KS 66612

Puckett, Micheal; The Blackburn Company, Inc., 2322 Tremont Dr., Suite 102, Baton Rouge, LA 70809

Quon, Mike; 53 Spring Street, New York, NY 10012

Ramirez, Luis E.; Laboratorio de Diseno y Analisis de Mercado S.A. Reforma 185 8o Piso Mexico 5, D.F.

Garcia, Andres; Laboratorio de Diseno y Analisis de Mercado S.A. Reforma 185 8o Piso Mexico 5, D.F.

Reid, Scott F.; 18 La Arcada Court, Santa Barbara, CA 93101

Rion & Ezquerro y Asociados S.C.; Calle de Santo Domingo 14, Plaza Molino de Santo Domingo, Tacubaya Mexico 18, D.F.

Rosentswieg, Gerry; The Graphic Studio, 8721 Beverly Boulevard, Los Angeles, CA

Roth, Randall R.; Roth Co., 535 North Michigan Ave., 2312 Chicago, IL 60611

Russell, Anthony; Anthony Russell Inc., 170 Fifth Avenue, New York, NY 10010

Sanjuan, Victor; Laboratorio de Diseno y Analisis de Mercado S.A. Reforma 185 8o Piso Mexico 5, D.F.

Scannell, Lynn; Emerson/Nichols/Bailey Inc., 1117 Merchants National Bank Building, Topeka, KS 66612

Segura Jr., Carlos M.; The Blackburn Company, Inc., 2322 Tremont Dr., Suite 102, Baton Rouge, LA 70809

Segura Jr., Carlos M.; Landmark Advertising Inc., 1256 Florida Blvd., Baton Rouge, LA 70802

Sellars, Don; Rice & Sellars, P.O. Box 342, Seattle, WA 98125

Sheldon Graphics; 7810 Paso Robles Ave. Van Nuys, CA 91406

Sierakowski, George; 2796 Marion St., Roseville, MN 55113

Skaggs, Steven; 546 Ridgecrest Rd. NE, Atlantic, GA 30307

Smith, Randall; 9191 Alvey Lane, Sandy, UT 84070

Sonderman, Joe; Design/Joe Sonderman Inc. 1209 Kenilworth Avenue, Charlotte, NC 28204

Spain, Carol; Fineline Graphics, 520 Norwood Dr., Hurst TX 76053

Spaulding, Denise; David E. Carter Corporate Communications, 1505 Carter Ave., P.O. Box 591 Ashland, KY 41101

Sposari, Jorge; Maclean & Sposari Comunicacion Visual, Eugenio Garza Sada 2258/2, Colonia Roma, Monterrey NL, Mexico

Sterrenburg, Don L.; 12004 Los Reyes Avenue, la Mirada, CA 90638

Sganzerla, Angelo; Via Anfossi 9, Milano, Italia

Sutherland, Humprey; Courtland Thomas White, 65 West 90th St., New York, NY 10024

Taft, Ron; Pen Reel, print/broadcast studio, 155 South Arlington Ave., Reno, NV 89501

Taylor, Winston; The Blackburn Company, Inc., 2322 Tremont Dr., Suite 102, Baton Rouge, LA 70809

Tolone, Diana G. de; Division de Carton y Papel de Mexico, S.A. de C.V.

Tweedy, Jim; Landmark Advertising Inc., 1256 Florida Blvd., Baton Rouge, LA 70802

Underwood, Eugene; The Diciduous Press, Box 527, Doylestown, PA 18901-0527

Urban, Timothy E.; Tim Urban Design, 2536 North 96th Street, Wauwatosa, WI 53226

Volinsky, Stan; Metropolitan Life Insurance Company, art dept., One Madison Ave., New York, NY 10010

Wahlberg, Charles J.; Wahlberg & Associates, 3101 Richmond Ave., Suite 224, Houston, TX 77098

Wallen, Arvid; Matrix Design Inc., 360 South Monroe, Suite 310, Denver CO 80209

Waller, Joseph D., 39 South Browning Rd., Somerdale, NJ 08083

White, Courtland Thomas, 65 West 90th St., New York, NY 10024

Wiens, Duane; Matrix Design Inc., 360 South Monroe, Suite 310, Denver, Co 80209

Wilson, Douglas; 2140 N. Lincoln Apt. 5202, Chicago, IL 60614

Wood, Alan; Alan Wood Graphic Design, 342 Madison Ave., Suite 1061, New York, NY 10017

Zahor, D. Bruce; Zahor Design Inc., 150 East 35th Street, New York, NY 10016